THE WISDOM OF SOCRATES

PHILOSOPHY OF HAPPINESS

THE WISDOM OF SOCRATES

PHILOSOPHY OF HAPPINESS

FERNAND SCHWARZ

NEW ACROPOLIS

Translated from the French edition published by New Acropolis France as *La Sagesse de Socrate: Philosophie du Bonheur.*

Translated by Gabriel Seoane

Cover Image Courtesy:

The Death of Socrates by Jacques Louis David, 1787.
The Metropolitan Museum of Art, New York.
Catharine Lorillard Wolfe Collection.
Source: The Met OA (www.metmuseum.org).

Published in 2025 by

NEW ACROPOLIS

Mumbai, India.
www.acropolis.org.in
mumbai@acropolis.org

ISBN: 978-81-964729-1-7

To the one whose presence has not left me

throughout the writing of this book

and whose patience and example put me

on the path of the eternal Socrates.

TABLE OF CONTENTS

PUBLISHER'S NOTE

Dear Reader,

It is a pleasure to present this book to you in its English translation. This treasure has been my companion for many years, allowing me to renew something essential in my philosophical journey. It is not the written words that enable this renewal, but the meaning they hold invites us to explore, reflect on, and express what takes root in both the mind and the heart.

This is a remarkable book, the essence of which is not really in the retelling of the life and ideas of a great philosopher, but is in its ability to present, in a clear and profound way, what living philosophy truly is, why it is essential, and what it can offer to humanity.

This is philosophy in its essence: transcendent and alive, far beyond a mere intellectual exchange of opinions. Philosophy is an approach to life and a state of consciousness that forms a bridge between heaven and earth. It enables the realisation of higher awareness and the attainment of happiness. True happiness is not conditioned by external possessions but is a characteristic of the authenticity of the individual, who is, at the same time, an integral part of the universe.

This little book reveals the role and character of the Teacher - both the one within us and the one outside us and, more importantly, the character of the Disciple-Philosopher. Few today can express these ideas as clearly and precisely as Fernand Schwarz does.

I hope this book will be an enjoyable and meaningful read for you.

Yaron Barzilay
National Director of New Acropolis India (North)

FOREWORD

I had the good fortune to meet Fernand Schwarz in 1979, and it would be an understatement to say that this encounter was a decisive moment in the history of my philosophical journey, in search of meaning, myself, and happiness.

This book is not, as one might expect, a summary of Socrates' life, nor yet another academic explanation of his philosophy. Socrates is present, of course, and even takes centre stage. But I would like to draw attention to how Socrates' wisdom brings to light the experience of happiness as something to be lived. And therein lies the difference!

To live is to experience in the present. It's about gleaning the essence of the lessons we learn from our life experiences. It means having the courage and capacity to grow in consciousness with constancy and enthusiasm, and to smile at life's challenges, because that is the very essence of being alive. Without this, without accepting the challenges, there is only survival. Happiness lies in the daily choice to live and the refusal to settle for mere survival.

And herein lies the genius of Fernand Schwarz - his ability to extract the essence of Socrates' philosophy and share it with us as a method of uniting and identifying with happiness. Please note that this is not a recipe to be applied more or less mechanically. Recipes should be left to the sophists. It is a method, and therefore a path of life, that needs to be built and rebuilt, step by step, day after day, by those who make the courageous choice to embark on it.

It's a luminous path, because happiness is not just the reward you receive at the end of the journey. Happiness is inherent in the act of walking the path - it's there from the start, from the moment you begin to move. It shines through in the luminosity of the path.

Fernand Schwarz transmits this light to us naturally, for he himself belongs to that 'small number' of souls who, as they walk the path, are able to identify with it and become the path itself. His words have the force of authentic personal example, and they speak to the heart and intuition of those who receive them.

His message is clear and obvious, simple without being oversimplified. When you reach the end of the reading and the reflection it inspires, you find yourself with a clear vision and a choice to make: the vision is that of the obvious – the happiness within our reach, or rather, within the reach of the virtue that each of us carries within ourselves. The choice is one of courage, essential to awaken to become just that: an awakened being, united with happiness.

Fernand Schwarz writes: "Happiness is the fruit of a decision. Let us decide to be happy and to continue to be so, by centering ourselves and maintaining that centre, by detaching ourselves from the centrifugal forces of conditioning, distractions and demands."

The greatest value of this book is undoubtedly that it radically changes our relationship with courage. Before reading it, it may seem that courage is beyond our reach, that it would be too much to ask, too hard, too demanding, and so we resign ourselves to a routine of survival and hope for a change that will come effortlessly from external circumstances. By the end of the book, courage seems a natural and indispensable response to nonsense. The reader is left with a new question: Why didn't he have the courage to choose happiness earlier?

Pierre Poulain
Founder of New Acropolis Israel

INTRODUCTION

Despite the twenty-five centuries that separate us from him, there is someone who remains timeless, continually rediscovered and perpetually new, because he embodies what is eternal and most profound in man: Socrates. Eternally questioned, and sometimes criticized, he is as relevant as ever. We cannot dismiss Socrates, for he exists within each of us.

Socrates lived in and fertilized the entire 5th century BCE - the age of Pericles, the golden age of Athens, a pivotal moment for all Western thought that continues to inspire the West. This was the moment when, unknowingly, Greek thought was preparing to conquer the world: Persia, India, the entire Mediterranean, the Roman Empire, and eventually, the whole of the West.

Socrates witnessed the end of one era - the age of physicist-philosophers and sophists. He ushered in another. After him, nothing remained the same. So much so, that even his contemporaries are referred to as pre-Socratic. He established philosophy as we understand it today.

Without taking himself too seriously, Socrates made philosophy both a science and a way of life – a practical knowledge. He taught an attitude of continuous learning, based on the application of knowledge that is constantly renewed. He opposed intellectualism, speaking of it as action devoid of meaning, and activism as utopia. His philosophy is a moral philosophy; he invented the field of Ethics.

Gradually, he developed a method - etymologically, the word method means *what puts one on the path* - rooted in his own life experiences. He used the difficulties and crises he faced to gain increasing self-mastery, even conquering the ultimate fear: Death. Rejecting the law of retaliation that divides and creates opposition, he introduced the West to dialogue, using dialectic as a method to trace a path to happiness through reason.

Thanks to him, philosophy became a means to access the highest wisdom, attainable only through an inner journey. Through philosophical language - a language accessible to reason - Socrates found a way to transmit teachings like Pythagoreanism and Orphism, previously reserved for the elite, and initiatic knowledge, like that which was disseminated in the Mysteries. He publicly expressed what many thought, but dared not to say, challenging the functioning of institutions and the behavior of individuals. Socrates rejected circular thinking, tirelessly fighting against the established singular way of thinking and all forms of hegemony. This ultimately led to his death sentence.

At a time when everyone sought happiness in the pursuit of power, material possessions, or social status, Socrates knew these pursuits could only bring fleeting satisfaction. He was the first public figure to declare their pursuit pointless and to decide to seek lasting happiness within himself.

For Socrates, the Good is not the result of an intellectual decree; it is a reality in itself. The intellect, through the practice of dialectic, helps one to understand and see the Good. One can then practice virtue and achieve happiness. Sophists developed techniques to dominate others. The contribution of Socrates is a path that allows one to conquer oneself and find happiness without it coming at the expense of others.

Socrates reminds us that true happiness is found within oneself. One can achieve it, by learning to look inward. This inner state allows one to face the difficulties and contradictions of existence and the apparent irony of destiny. In fact, it enables one to reconcile seemingly incompatible opposites by understanding and treating them as complementary - for example, how to remain serene, even happy, in adverse circumstances. This reveals the true scope of love, not as a force for procreation, but as a unifying force through which unity is expressed.

To attain happiness, one must stop being a prisoner of oneself and liberate the soul through practical knowledge, which are the virtues. Far from being sanctimonious or boring, to which they have been reduced, virtues are, in fact, an effective way to attain happiness.

Socrates' life demonstrates that human beings are not doomed to be victims of fate; one can take control of one's destiny. He did not wait for happiness to fall from the sky; he forged it. Because he is not a loser, but a winner, he overturned the model of the Greek tragic hero. Socrates is the pioneer of a philosophy of enthusiasm.

CHAPTER 1

THE THREE CRISES OF SOCRATES

Socrates left no writings, but everyone who had the chance to know him, friend or foe, was deeply impressed by his peculiar character: the ugliest man in Athens, yet the one with the most beautiful soul. Although the mystery surrounding him will probably never be solved, his closeness and relevance to us are astonishing. Everyone can identify with him through his way of being and acting - his naturalness, the crises he went through, his irony, and his apparent nonconformity.

But Socrates was not made in a day. In fact, his method, which later inspired Plato's Dialectic, was born from crises, his ability to overcome, and the fundamental learnings and decisive actions that he drew from them. It is because he does not know everything, because he suffers and struggles to transcend his own suffering without being swept away by life's circumstances, that Socrates becomes particularly endearing and a true guide for our minds.

The Time of Socrates

Socrates (470-399 BCE) lived in the 5th century BCE, an astonishing pivotal period that brought the city of Athens to the pinnacle of Greek civilization. It was the century of Pericles, the century of the construction of the Parthenon built by the architect Ictinos, the century of the most accomplished art of sculptor Phidias, painter Apelles, and the sacred theater of Aeschylus, Sophocles, and Euripides; the latter was a close friend of Socrates.

It was a very special moment that saw the birth of a new world. The Persians, who had been at war with the Greek city-states since the beginning of the century, were defeated and had retreated to Asia. Europe would never become a satrapy.[1] But the taste of victory was bitter. Tens of thousands of Greek citizens fell on the battlefields, the ancient Greek monarchies were exhausted, cities were depopulated, and many families destroyed. The confrontation between the Greek city-states and Persia was the equivalent of a true world war at the time. The situation was somewhat similar to that of Europe at the beginning of the 20th century, at the end of the First World War, when it faced the challenge of creating a new political and cultural order on the old continent.

In the 5th century BCE a wave of social, moral, and cultural reconstruction offered unprecedented opportunities to the less conformist minds, who were eager for new responsibilities.

Pericles modified the government system of Athens and established democracy. Greek city-states relaunched maritime trade and dominated the Mediterranean, gradually conquering the known world. Expansion was continuous, and the number of colonies constantly increased. A new taste for freedom developed, associated with the need to express oneself in original forms.

History accelerated. Only a century separated Socrates from Alexander, who in 326 BCE reached the banks of the Indus, thereby uniting the East and the West. He chose Babylon as his capital, thus beginning the Hellenistic period, which would become the origin of the cultural melting pot of the Middle East and the future Byzantine world.

In 5th-century Athens, Socrates fertilized minds and contributed to the birth of this new world. He rejected all forms of dogmatism, claimed to have no teaching to impart, presented himself as a "midwife of ideas", enabling his disciples to find the truth within themselves if they were capable. As a catalyst for truth, Socrates was not a teacher who transmitted theories but a master who allowed everyone to confront themselves. He had the art of disarming his interlocutor when least expected, triggering a process through which, if the individual's nature allowed, they could experience the truth; the truth that everyone carries within themselves.

Socrates and Women

Socrates was born into a modest family of free citizens. His mother, Phaenarete, was a midwife, and his father,

Sophroniscus, a little-known sculptor. Socrates, who never accepted money for his teachings and always earned his living through his work, learned the trade of sculpting from his father. But from his youth, he trained in the art of not only sculpting stone but also sculpting the mind.

There are numerous accounts of several encounters that were decisive for him; the first of which was to do with his mother, who knew half of Athens and assisted in the childbirth of high society women. She taught him the love of life, the art of bringing life into the world. She also taught him that all men are born the same way. She had the gift of healing and knew the art of treating with plants. It was through her that Socrates discovered the magical force of nature and the love of life.

For an Athenian of his time, Socrates' behavior was atypical: he was not misogynistic. At that time, a wife's primary function was to bear children and she was kept away from important conversations. Banquets and social gatherings were generally held among men. Only certain high-level courtesans with intellectual and cultural sophistication and a certain beauty, the *hetairai*, were admitted to these meetings. One of them, Aspasia, stood out and became the companion of Pericles, who lived with her until his death, honoring her as a true lady. Aspasia had created a small school of rhetoric and logic in Pericles' house for a select circle. The friendship between Pericles and Socrates allowed the latter to enter this circle.

The teaching of rhetoric develops the art of thinking well and expressing oneself in a manner that can be understood, fosters discernment, uncovers unsuspected facets of reality, and develops a taste for investigation. Through Aspasia, Socrates understood that humans are not bound to suffer life as if it were fated; the laws of nature do not bind us to the point of stifling the soul; though we are not perfect, we are perfectible. Moreover, Aspasia revealed to him the force of love as a motor for perfection, while for the sophists, the need for perfection generally stemmed from the desire for appearances, the taste for power, and the need to dominate and prove one's superiority. Socrates discovered that the path to perfecting oneself, is beneficial, not only for oneself, but also for all those around us. Perfection then, is pursued for the love of others, and for that which is superior to us. Thus, it is possible to escape both the resignation to fate and the law of the survival of the fittest.

In 440 BCE, Pericles summoned the great priestess of Apollo from the Temple of Bassae, Diotima of Mantinea, to lead the purification ceremonies in Athens, which had been ravaged by a plague epidemic. Diotima lived in seclusion in the sanctuary of Apollo Epicurius in the legendary and inhospitable region of Arcadia. She served Apollo Epicurius (The Helpful, The Healer), who purified and cleansed inner impurities, and whose arrow struck straight to the heart. The arrows of Apollo Epicurius targeted only the impurities that prevented the experience of selfless love, destroying inner blindness and untamed passion through purification.

The impact of the priestess on the young Socrates seeking perfection at the time, would be irreversible. Diotima taught him the role of love in attaining the contemplation of the highest truths. She initiated him into the mysteries of celestial

Eros of the Orphic tradition.[2] Eros is the force that reconciles differences, unites opposites by allowing the circulation of life throughout the universe. It is the need that drives one to seek the unknown, to transcend oneself by ascending from human to divine love: the *epopteia*[3] of the Mysteries.

Thanks to Diotima, Socrates realized that knowledge is not intellectual but a way to purge passions. The knowledgeable human gains inner clarity, a light of his own, that endures beyond the turmoil of circumstances.

By the age of forty, Socrates gradually freed himself of worldly concerns through reason and love. From the naturalism of previous thinkers who focused on the study of the laws of physics, he moved towards humanism. He distanced himself from the sophists he opposed. Purifying his thought, he evolved towards philosophy.

Fighting for Athens

Like every Greek citizen, Socrates fought for his city until the age of sixty. Three times he went to the battlefront, carrying a spear and shield, and saved the lives of notable figures like Alcibiades and Xenophon. As a man of combat outside the city when circumstances required it, he rejected violence in civilian life, where for him, the fight was solely on a moral plane.

Socrates challenged citizens in public spaces: "Stop, my friend, and let's talk a bit. Not about a truth I hold, not about the hidden essence of the world, but about what you were going to do when I met you. You believed it was just, or beautiful, or good, since you were going to do it; explain to me what justice, beauty, goodness are."[4]

He shook up passersby with his questions, irritating them as well. One day, exasperated, someone struck him. Socrates looked at him and said: "There are days in Athens when one doesn't know how to dress to go out - with or without a helmet!" On another occasion, he was kicked, and his disciples urged him to press charges. "If a donkey kicked me, would it occur to me to file a complaint?" Socrates replied in the presence of his aggressor. He became a well-known figure, questioning everyone, eager to educate the young aristocrats destined for power. Among them was a young man of great beauty; the physically and intellectually talented Alcibiades, who could have succeeded Pericles. For almost twenty years, Socrates tried to awaken him, encouraging him to progress morally and spiritually. But Alcibiades preferred the path of appearances, military activity, competition, and politics.[5] Later, when Athens needed him most, Alcibiades would betray his homeland. Disappointment gripped Socrates, who was already in his fifties; the one in whom he had placed his trust and hope was not prepared to follow the path he had taught, the path leading to Being and renouncing all possessions other than possessing oneself.

His disciple's ambition for power and rejection of virtue led to the first crisis of Socrates.

The Break with Alcibiades: First Crisis

Faced with his failure as a teacher, Socrates decided to part ways with his disciple, leaving him to his own tendencies:

play, pleasure, social validation, power. This crisis led Socrates to a relentless introspection. He isolated himself, plunged into deep melancholy, and meditated on the necessity of becoming humbler. He realized that virtue could not be transmitted, that each must seek it for themselves, that no one can live it for another, and that one cannot help someone who does not want to help themselves. For Socrates, virtue was a constant disposition to do good and to avoid doing harm. He associated the concept of love with knowledge and moral virtue.

He understood that his own pride caused him to believe that he could eradicate the root of evil, and that his own example of virtue could lead his disciple to love it enough to practice it himself: "As for me, I do not possess any knowledge that I have taught and in which I would have done this man a service. However, I believed that by living with him, I could make him a better person through love."[6]

He concluded that to resolve his crisis, he must behave with greater humility and cease to offer his services to any single beneficiary or chosen individual; instead to dispense it to all. He vowed to seek people, especially the young, where they were, in the streets of Athens. "My only concern is to go back and forth to persuade you, young and old, to have no greater or equal concern for your body and fortune, than you must have about how to make your soul the best it can be, and to say to you: 'It is not from riches that virtue comes, but it is from virtue that riches and all other goods come, for individuals as well as for the State'."[7] And as Françoise Hellmann aptly summarizes: "I am the gadfly that will never cease to awaken you."[8]

Socrates would not abandon or betray this mission of awakening the consciousness of people, for anything in the world.[9]

The Oracle of Delphi: Second Crisis

In 420 BCE, Socrates was fifty years old. His friend Chaerephon, who loved him dearly, was appointed by Athens to lead the procession to consult the oracle at Delphi on behalf of the city. Chaerephon took the opportunity to ask the oracle a question that had troubled him for years: "Who is the wisest man in Athens?" The oracle replied, "Sophocles is wise, Euripides is wiser, but Socrates is the wisest of all men."[10] Chaerephon was satisfied. The answer was recorded on the Delphic tablets. And Socrates would finally be recognized! When he returned to Athens and reported the oracle's response to Socrates, the latter was stunned: it marked the beginning of his second crisis. He experienced a new bout of dejection, unable to comprehend what had happened. He rejected the oracle's words and sank into a long silence.

When he emerged from his dejection, he proposed to test the oracle.[11] Thus, he was seen going from house to house, questioning Athens' wisest and most knowledgeable: painters, architects, military officers, priests. He conversed with all those who had mastered various disciplines and asked them, "Please, will you enlighten me with your wisdom and advice?" Flattered to be asked by Socrates, they all puffed up and proclaimed their own truths.[12] But Socrates continued to interrogate them until they gradually doubted their own knowledge, demonstrating that they actually did not know, what they thought they knew. Many did not appreciate discovering that they are ignorant! This would prove fatal to Socrates, as we will see later.

Eventually, he overcame his crisis and understood what the Oracle had meant. He realized that it did not mean he possessed the most encyclopedic knowledge in Athens; his wisdom lay in knowing that he was ignorant, giving rise to the famous declaration, "I know that I know nothing."[13] The "wise" didn't know, that they did not know. Knowing of his ignorance, he could improve himself. Knowing what he didn't know, indicated where to search.

Once again, through the Oracle of Delphi, Apollo showed Socrates the way. The famous maxim inherited from the Mysteries was inscribed on the pediment of the Temple of Apollo at Delphi: "Know Thyself, and Thou shall know the Universe and the Gods." To achieve this, Socrates established the practice of inner dialogue by which to triumph over ignorance. Socrates was wise due to his awareness of not being wise; thanks to this feeling of lacking wisdom, a deep love for it awakened. This is the literal meaning of the word "philosophy": love of wisdom, of truth.

Socrates resolved his crisis by definitively incarnating as a philosopher and fighting the sophists more than ever.

The Sophists

Citizen assemblies replaced the old monarchies that ruled the Greek city-states. The fragmentation of the aristocracy gave way to new political currents. Democracy took hold, and a party system emerged. The Greek city-state (polis) brought forth new political systems to govern social life.

In this changing world, the need to train orators capable of persuading public opinion grew. Anyone desiring to take the reins of power and manage state affairs had to learn rhetoric, the art of arguing and debating to defeat their opponents. Educating adolescents from prominent families who aspired for power became a state affair. This new "market" was occupied by sophists, a term that originally meant "eminent sage", a kind of professorial authority. Today, we might call them "intellectuals".

Over time, sophists became primarily known for providing techniques to win arguments. Their goal was not to teach the truth about Man but to equip young people with the necessary means to win in any situation. They were concerned, not with seeking the truth, but with demonstrating that they are right.[14] They denied the possibility of defining the Good, as they believed it varied according to individuals, social categories, and ethnic origins.

Socrates contradicted them because he believed in a universal Good, the source of all particular goods. Initiation into the knowledge of this Good, according to him, provided everyone with the true means to discern the right action in any given situation, through an investigation that allowed one to encounter their inner being and act in the light of universal principles.

The agnostic sophists abandoned the idea of relating knowledge with metaphysics, and made the human being into a god, who did not need ethical, cathartic, and spiritual values. For them, what was important was not to conquer oneself, but to defeat opponents and obtain the benefits of temporal satisfactions.

The sophists' vision was utilitarian. They taught their students to use the State to satisfy personal interests by using the art of arousing emotions and passions. What interested them was effectiveness. They used any means to achieve their goals. Unlike their predecessors, the physicist-philosophers, they were not concerned with understanding the laws of nature, believing that nature was driven by capricious forces and that man-made laws were mere conventions established according to the interests of those in power. From the realization of a truth - the impermanence of all that is manifested - the sophists introduced cultural and moral relativism into Greek society. Through his fight against the sophists, Socrates, as reported by Aristotle, established the idea of a universal definition which embraces all that is defined, because it reaches the universal essence through particular examples. In a way, he imposed the scientific framework and the vision of unity beyond diversity.

But even more important for Socrates was the idea that it is better to suffer injustice than to commit it.[15] With this paradox, he founded the definition of human dignity, and it was the same paradox that led to his third crisis.

Dying for Athens: Third Crisis

Socrates identified the Beautiful, that is, the morally good, with the pleasant and useful, and the ugly, that is, the morally bad, with what causes pain and harm. According to Socrates, the worst of all evils is not death but ceasing to philosophize, in other words, ceasing to seek and do good.[16] These values led to the fatal outcome of his life.

His first crisis led to examination of consciousness, the second to dialogue as a way of purifying ignorance. This time, he had to confront the essence of his teaching: living according to his principles and demonstrating the superiority of the spirit over matter and the immortality of the soul.

The third crisis occurred at the end of his life, during the famous trial of Socrates. In 399 BCE, although the tyranny of the oligarchs had fallen, the democratic party governing the city introduced new forms of terror. Any citizen could accuse another. Unfortunately, Pericles had been dead for thirty years and his legacy had passed into the hands of incompetent magistrates within the city's administrative body, who participated in widespread corruption. The 'gadfly' of Athens' consciousness, Socrates, was a major inconvenience for them.[17]

One of the "elder sages" of Athens, Anytus, used the pretext of feeling offended by Socrates' irreverence and irony towards the social and religious conventions of the time. He persuaded the young Meletus to begin a trial against Socrates to defend the public good and cleanse the city of those who were corrupting the youth and mocking the city's gods. Socrates was accused of the crimes of impiety and immorality.

Given the nature of the charges, these two offenses were judged not by the civil court of Areopagus, but by the Archon[18] and the *heliasts*, the judges responsible for handling crimes against the state. Hence, Socrates faced the death penalty.

During the trial, Socrates faced a harsh truth: he could do nothing more for Athens. He had fought for his city, and had given it as many citizens governed by wisdom as possible. Yet it had condemned him, accusing him of the worst evils. He wanted to awaken Athens, but he was accused of corrupting its youth and violating its laws. The city he loved so much could not reform itself from within; it did not produce philosophers or virtuous individuals. On the contrary, it evolved towards totalitarianism. What good was it to be proclaimed the wisest man in Athens if he could do nothing for it? Compared to this failure, his experience with Alcibiades was nothing. Since he could not live for Athens, Socrates would die for it. He did nothing to save himself from the trial or the death sentence. He walked alone towards the terrible confrontation of living by the law and dying by it. He accepted death, to gain immortality. Conquering the fear of death is the best way to prepare in life. This is the essence of *maieutics*, the art of being born from oneself, through the death of ignorance, pride, and intellectualism within oneself.

Why was Socrates accused of impiety? As Plato recounts in the dialogue with the priest Euthyphro, Socrates opposed not religion, but superstition. He condemned the tradition of Greek mythology that anthropomorphized the gods, presenting them as beings subject to passions, destroying each other. He did not believe that the relationship between gods and humans was an exchange of favors. For Socrates, true piety was to be one with justice. Since both humans and the gods were of divine essence, the relationship between them was to be established by cultivating harmony. Justice could not be commercialized.

That said, the Greek religion of that time was primarily social; deities protected the city and its customs. They maintained cohesion among citizens but did not concern themselves with the destiny of individuals. Although Socrates respected and followed the city's rites, he believed they were unconcerned with the becoming of the individual as such... In reality, he did not introduce new social deities into the Greek pantheon but explained that the only god we can individually contact is our own immortal soul, the famous *daimon*, the inspiring genius, the inner voice, that signals what one should not do. It is this semi-divine voice, behind which lies the inner god, that allows each person to be One with the Whole.

In reality, the "new god" Socrates introduced to Athens was the individual consciousness, the foundation of inner freedom and human dignity. It was this god that the court of Athens disputed, and which Socrates could not renounce.[19]

According to Socrates, the state must fundamentally be concerned with educating its citizens, and ensuring its magistrates are examples of virtue.[20] Over time, the institutions founded by Pericles, based on virtues of moderation, rigor, and balance, transformed into an immense bureaucratic machine with an ever-increasing annual budget to maintain Athens' administration. During the thirty years following the death of Pericles, the government of Athens was in the hands of different parties, each destroying what the predecessor had done.

Socrates did not criticize the state as such, but the system of passion, corruption, and bureaucracy that hindered the true development of free and equal citizens before the law. This is what he warned the youth about.

Although the Archon and city magistrates conducted the trial, the real judges and the members of the popular courts of Athens were the *heliasts*. The number of these citizen jurors varied depending on the type of judgment to be carried out. They were recruited from among citizens over thirty who enjoyed full civil rights and expressed a desire to be *heliasts*. However, they could not hold multiple positions, meaning they could not simultaneously be part of the Council of 55, the real executive assembly of Athens. They also could not be public arbitrators, police magistrates, lead wars, be agents of the treasury, or hold truly high and important positions. Wealthy citizens also abstained from this role, preferring to attend to their own affairs. This is why, even in the time of Pericles, it was decided to compensate jurors for their duty.

Consequently, over time jurors were either senile old men, poorly educated citizens, or peasants for whom the compensation supplemented their lost harvests during wartime. Lacking true autonomy of judgment and personal means, they could be greatly influenced by the ruling powers. Five hundred and one popular jurors were randomly selected for Socrates' trial, and their vote would decide his life.

Like other philosophers and satirical authors of the time, Socrates called for a reform of the judicial system because many Greeks considered the judiciary the very heart of the city. He warned against the danger of justice, which hiding behind democracy, serves a handful of tyrants. Young Athenians, including some of the brightest minds like the young Plato, who was in his twenties when he met Socrates, followed him into the streets, supporting his ideal of judicial reform. They mainly denounced the incompetence, lack of qualification of those holding public office, which in the medium term, would lead Athens from democracy to tyranny, as history had proven. Socrates' popular success and impact on the young people were interpreted as an attempt to corrupt the youth.

"It is of their own accord that young people from the wealthiest families, who have the most leisure, attach themselves to me for the pleasure of hearing the people I am refuting, and often they try to imitate me, try their hand at testing others in turn. Needless to say, I imagine, they find plenty of people who think they know something, but know very little, or nothing. As a result, the people that these young men refuted, get angry and have turned against me, and spread the rumor that there is a certain Socrates, a vile fellow who corrupts the youth. When asked what Socrates does and teaches, they have nothing to say and are embarrassed... Since they undoubtedly care about their reputation, as they are aggressive and many in number and speak vehemently and persuasively, they have long filled your ears with vehement slander. It is based on these slanders that Meletus, along with Anytus and Lycon, attacked me - Meletus represents the poets' hostility, Anytus that of the tradesmen, and Lycon that of the orators, i.e. the political leaders."[21]

"Know well that if you condemn me to death, it is not I - if I am truly the man I claim to be - who will suffer the greatest harm, but rather you yourselves. Neither Meletus nor Anytus can harm me in any way. How could they, since it is not permitted, I imagine, for someone of lesser worth to harm someone of greater worth? Oh, no doubt, an accuser may succeed in having me condemned to death, exiled, or stripped of my civil rights, as they or others might view these to be grave misfortunes, but I do not share that view. On the contrary, I consider it much more serious to act as they are doing now, trying to unjustly condemn a man to death. Now, Athenians, it is not my defense I am presenting, far from it, but yours; I fear that by condemning me, you might harm yourselves more than me by rejecting the gift the god has given you."[22]

The jury found Socrates guilty; 281 to 220 votes.

According to tradition, the law did not fix the penalty, but a second vote determined the choice of penalties from among those proposed by the prosecution and the defense. The jury could choose either. Since the prosecution had already demanded the death penalty, it was up to the defense to propose an alternative sanction such as exile or loss of civil rights to commute the death sentence. But Socrates did not want to take advantage of this opportunity. He considered himself innocent and thus proposed no penalty, leaving the jury no choice but to condemn him to death. Preserving his integrity, he preferred death, leaving his judges to face their own conscience.

Socrates had always adhered to the public decisions of the city. As a good citizen, how could he love Athens without her laws? If he were exiled or lost his civil rights, he would cease to be a citizen, a free man. He preferred to die free, rather than live deprived of rights.

The conclusion of Socrates' trial coincided with the Festival of Apollo at Delos, temporarily delaying the execution of his death sentence. Once again, Apollo had intervened in Socrates' life, giving him the opportunity to convey his deepest message. While in prison, he taught his disciples who visited him, about the immortality of the soul,[23] the nobility needed when exiting life, and the happiness of being a philosopher and feeling eternally young.

In May and June 399 BCE, the sacred boat of Apollo returned to Athens. Its sails turned westward, announcing the beginning of Socrates' journey to Hades, the realm of the dead. He consoled his disciples and withdrew to the prison dormitory. His mortal life slowly ended with sips of hemlock. Although terror was unleashed against those who, filled with love for their master, had accompanied him to the end, Socrates' words survived through the works of all those who were irreversibly inspired by Socrates' *daimon*.

Even today, the heart of Socrates lives on in all who fight for justice and dignity, and ardently seek to discover the human essence within themselves.

CHAPTER 2

THE SOCRATIC METHOD: DIALECTIC

"As long as there are philosophers, they cannot ignore the perpetual rebirth of Socratic questioning. And they will plunge into his infinite game to better savour its strange and astonishing vitality." —*Anne Baudart*[1]

The term "method", derived from Greek literally means "approach" and implies the idea of finding a path. It is a process, consisting of an itinerary, a journey, under the auspices and inspiration of Hermes, the god of crossroads, commerce, and the path of knowledge, leading to the discovery of an appropriate answer. Each of Socrates' crises operated as a messenger of the god of knowledge, guiding him back on the right path. But what path was he seeking? The path leading to himself. His crises prompted him to forge this path.

Selfless and without egoism, Socrates' method aimed to help each individual find their own path and law of action.

Aware of his own imperfections, Socrates continually sought self-improvement. He did not place himself on a pedestal as one who knows; instead, he challenged his own ignorance daily to move forward. In doing so, he embraced the apparent contradiction of practicing a knowledge or technique he had not yet fully mastered. His way of life embodied a philosophy of assumed risk. He did not fall into the psychological trap of acting only when he believed he knew everything and the risk was zero, which is precisely what prevents many people, paralyzed by the perfectionism syndrome, from taking action. Without confrontation, one cannot learn or improve in anything.

Socrates understood that one can never be fully prepared for action through theory alone, and that in reality what prepares one, is the decision to act, while being aware of one's own imperfections, and learning from experimentation, whether we win or lose. According to Socrates, success lies in having the courage and intelligence to confront one's fears and doubts, in overcoming them.

In summary, one could define this method as the simultaneous development of investigation and practice, in the pursuit of wisdom. This involves accepting an in-depth dialogue with oneself, between one's thoughts and actions.

The Art of Dialogue

Socratic wisdom consists in knowing how to do good. But this is not simple, as it is not easy to know what is good or bad for oneself or others. How to reconcile what is good for one with what is good for all? How to act in a way that does not do harm while seeking to do good?

Socrates invites us to unite knowledge with love to enter into dialogue with people. Etymologically, dialogue means the exchange of words or discourse (*logoi*) through the intellectual and physical space separating two people (*dia*). Dialogue does not exist without at least two people, and is established in the space "between" things. It is an art of making connections.

According to Socrates, the master does not necessarily know more than the disciple, and practices investigation like the disciple, and with the disciple. The true relationship between master and disciple consists of a common effort to seek the truth.

The master has experience and greater technical mastery of investigation, in the art of asking questions.[2] It is not knowing more that makes someone a master, but the ability to accompany someone else in their quest for truth and to bring them face to face with themselves.

Dialogue is not a technique, linked to situations, and proceeding through inquiries and explanations. It is the essential expression of a joint effort to reveal a shared inner truth. The master is not someone who transmits a type of knowledge to a more or less receptive student; he does not teach through monologues. The relationship established through dialogue is that of two individuals communicating with each other; two consciousnesses practicing investigation and entering into a relationship, in order to attain a common truth.

The disciple always gives the master the opportunity to better understand him. Pierre Hadot reminds us that questioning the individual through dialogue leads one to decide whether they will truly commit to live in accordance with their consciousness and reason. The very foundation of the individual's actions is challenged. They become aware that they are themselves the living question. Socrates urges them "to care less about what they have and more about what they are," and to remember that, "haste is the sign of those who want to escape from themselves."[3]

Quoting Jean Lacroix, one can say that through dialogue, "one no longer forces the other to think like oneself but strives to convince them to agree freely, if they so desire. While dialogue signals the transition from the individual to the universal, it also recognizes the freedom of the other... those who cannot engage in dialogue are fanatics; they are ignorant of who they are and of who the others are. Dialogue is the advent of philosophy, which is non-violence."[4]

Accepting dialogue means to embrace the possibility of moving toward a common destiny through different paths. It is about sharing an invisible presence through a visible relationship between two people because truth arises "between" those who engage in dialogue.

When this relationship is established, something occurs that written words cannot fully convey. Indeed, when two or more beings participate in the same vision, the presence of That arises in the plane they occupy. In other words, beyond, and independent of, the words expressed in an exchange, involving both feelings and gestures, the bonds woven through dialogue allow the manifestation of a transcendent truth - a shared idea, knowledge, or feeling. This truth lies within and at the very heart of, the space created by the relationship. The magic of the relationship allows the manifestation of a third element, that includes itself in the relationship, and shares itself. An intangible good is made perceptible, which as soon as the exchange ceases, returns to the invisible. When dialogue becomes internal, the magic persists and the connection remains intact. Once this link to oneself is established, it cannot be broken. One then reaches the stage that all traditions speak of, which is to learn from silence, from the essence beyond appearances.

Sharing this truth makes it come alive and rejuvenates those who share it. "The task of dialogue consists (paradoxically) essentially in demonstrating the limits of language, the impossibility of language to fully communicate moral and existential experience... Socratic philosophy is... awakening of consciousness, accession to a level of being that can only be realized in a person-to-person relationship."[5]

Dialectic: A Journey of the Soul

The method invented by Socrates is dialectic: the art of bringing two seemingly contradictory discourses into dialogue to access a higher truth.[6] Through a gradual play of questions, Socrates dismantles the false knowledge of his interlocutor.[7] A true instrument of testing and critique, dialectic does not settle for the plausible or probable but unveils appearances and any pretense of truth.

Through progressive effort and the practice of rigor, dialectic also has a positive application: it avoids hasty or random conclusions. It elevates the participants of the dialogue to intuit the essence, dissipating all false quarrels.

It is a method of thought that subjects discourse to the test of principles of logic. It compels the philosopher to demonstrate both the internal coherence of their discourse as well as its compatibility with reality.

Socrates is not content with knowing; he seeks to understand, and questions the sciences he studies. Dialectic seeks the meaning of what is studied. Through this attitude, true philosophies access a dimension broader than specialized sciences do. The ultimate ascent demanded by dialectic is not about seeking an intellectual intuition of truth but about attaining a comprehensive vision of reality (in Greek, *synoptica*) in order to place this science at the service of man.

Thought, or dialogue with oneself, arises from the awareness of logical inconsistencies in discourse. True knowledge, according to Socrates, does not consist in possessing the truth but in knowing how to methodically construct, through logical processes of unification, the dialectical ascent towards the simple - or analysis-synthesis to find a truth - and then apply it in a dialectical descent towards the multiple.

Dialectic allows us to free ourselves from sensory appearance and finds causes or essences. It liberates the soul from the pretense of the sensations; the pretense that they are the origins, or the causes, of truth. Once clarity is attained, it also allows the soul to descend, unburdened from the influence of its environment and appearances, to act in reality. The practice of dialectic helps the soul construct the path that allows it to move freely across the different planes of existence. Dialectic proposes a dual path, a round-trip. By the ascending path, one arrives at the definition and the knowledge of what is spoken; the descending path verifies-demonstrates.

The Ascending Path: Analogy

Analogy, the science of relationships - from the Greek *ana* (implying movement and repetition) and *logos* (meaning relationship) - consists of the repetition of an identical relationship, such that the relationship remains the same, while the plane changes. The ascending path or dialectical ascension is that of synthesis, achieved through the functions of analogy. Analogy establishes a relationship between ideas and objects. The well-known example given by Plato is that of a craftsman who wants to build a bed. To do this, he must first enter into a relationship with the idea of a bed, by representing it mentally. Plato explains that the bed made by the craftsman will be in the image of this idea; in other words, it will be an analogous version on the level of the empirical world, of a reality that exists on the intelligible plane.[8]

Analogy helps to understand the relationship between the part and the whole. It allows us to move away from the sensible plane and turn towards the intelligible plane. Intelligence cannot function without analogy because it goes further than understanding things through reason alone. It involves the ability to discern the relationships that things establish between themselves: it is not the same thing to perceive sounds or colors on the one hand, and a piece of music or a painting on the other. Plato insists, by recalling, that looking at a finger does not awaken intelligence. A finger is just a finger, but if one observes the thumb and the index finger, they will notice that the index is a long finger because it is comparatively longer than the thumb. If one then looks at the index and middle fingers, one will conclude that the index finger is short because it is shorter than the middle finger. At first glance, it is impossible to understand that the index finger can be both long and short. Sensory testimony here contravenes the principle of non-contradiction; in other words, reason alone cannot comprehend contradictory elements.[9] Only the work of intelligence makes it possible to resolve the contradiction and understand that long and short are relative, and arise from relationships, from analogies.

Analogy provides a cognitive function that allows one to rise from the sensible to the intelligible, and facilitates the ascent. The prefix *ana* not only indicates repetition but also the idea of a movement from bottom to top, and designates the movement of return to the origin.

Analogy also has an educational and didactic function because images or symbols make it possible to communicate messages or meanings relating to other planes of reality: for example, the flight of a bird can also signify freedom.

Analogy is the faculty of intelligence that allows to establish links. It is the basis of creativity, the principle of which is to establish links between things that seemed unrelated. The art of creating links frees from compartmentalization as it allows fluid communication between things. Analogy brings a new vision of the same things.

The Descending Path: Dieresis or Verification in Multiplicity

The second phase of the dialectical movement is the descending dialectic or dieresis, from the Greek *diairesis* (division). It involves subjecting the synthesis achieved during the dialectical ascent to the test of the apparent dichotomy, the opposition in the empirical world.

After reducing multiple empirical acts to the unity of a principle, one must verify if the discovered criterion is truly discriminating and whether it corresponds to a general law. This is why it must be applied in multiplicity and tested to see if it can characterize different objects and particular events likely to respond to a universal law. It is the confrontation of thought with the concrete world. Thus, for a scientific law to be valid, it must have no exceptions: the law of gravity is a law because it applies to all bodies.

The dialectical approach can be illustrated by how Socrates approaches the notion of virtue, showing that it is "one through its particular expressions."[1C]

To Meno and Protagoras, who defend the idea that there is a swarm of virtues, Socrates responds, "There are also swarms of bees. The way to know what virtue is may not be very different from that of defining the bee. Bees are numerous, virtues too; bees are of various species, and so are virtues; bees differ from each other, and virtues as well. But bees, diverse in size, beauty, and other characteristics, all resemble each other as bees, and what they share in common makes them all bees together and makes each one a bee in each swarm. Similarly, however numerous and diverse virtues may be, they all share a common characteristic, and it is this common characteristic that makes each one a virtue in a swarm of virtues."[11] For Socrates, the form common to all virtues is wisdom, just as their opposites have thoughtlessness in common.

The Dual Movement of the Soul

The dialectical journey leads, as we will see later, to inner happiness, like the spiral ascent of a pilgrim to the summit of Mount Helicon. Through this one sheds all false questions, and, once at the summit, comes to an understanding and inspiration regarding one's quest. There, one encounters the Muses, inspirers of sciences and arts. It is contact with these higher sources, representing the summit of one's own consciousness, that allows benefiting from a clear vision. This is the dialectical ascent.

When descending from Mount Helicon, the pilgrim is a different person. He has shed a part of his ignorance; he purifies and simplifies himself. The material encountered during the descent becomes the means to translate what was understood. It is the same as that which was encountered during the ascent, but the new clarity allows for finding their use and concrete application with greater accuracy. His relationship now, with the material is different.

The dual dialectical movement confirms that the nature of reality is both One and Multiple, which, though seemingly contradictory, is actually complementary. "The road up and the road down are one and the same." This formula from Heraclitus illustrates the principle of transformation of things, of alternation between involution and evolution. In truth, everything is contemporaneous, but appears separate because we live in time. Reality, however, is both inside and outside of time. To situate oneself at its level is to attain unity and find happiness. Transformation governs the nature of exchanges, such as commerce, war, or dialectic. From this exchange emerges justice, allowing the right tension between forces, the harmonization of opposites. Justice connects what ascends and descends.

The Socratic method rejects all forms of exclusion or separatism. It embraces the natural law of polarity that governs the universe: day and night, cold and heat, masculine and feminine. Through its logic of inclusion, it transforms pairs of opposites into the union of contraries.

Through dialectic as a method allowing the intelligence (in Greek, *nous*), the seat of our immortality, to perceive the truth residing in the "heaven" (the world of ideas) and to apply and practice the good on earth (the sensible world), Socrates provides a philosophical framework for the ancestral Greek belief in the dual movement of the soul, a true bridge between heaven and earth. He offers a practical manner for those who wish to live by elevating their soul and act in accordance with their innermost conviction.

He frees man from mere belief, providing a path of realization through one's own action and thought. But to be able to descend and ascend successfully between the plane of ideas, of archetypes, and that of objects and images, the path is narrow, and it is very easy to deviate and make mistakes. Whether starting an ascent or verifying the realization of an idea in the concrete world, one must respect, to the extent of one's capability, the three phases of the dialectical method.

The Three Phases of the Dialectical Method

Dialectic is not the knowledge but the method that leads to it. Socrates gives us the courage to confront our own ignorance by marking the path. Knowledge is at the heart of the path. It is the dialogue established along the way that reveals the truth. Through the practice of dialectic, Socrates invites us to participate in a true alchemical process.

Like alchemical work, dialectic has three phases:

- Exhortation or Protreptic
- Refutation *(elegkhos)*
- Maieutics or self-birth (birthing oneself)

These three phases indicate a spiral evolutionary process illustrated by the ascent of the famous Mount Helicon mentioned earlier, at the summit of which reside the nine Muses, with the goal that the soul return to the light of the origin.

But in daily life, the three phases also constitute a cycle of renewal and improvement, enabling us to become better each day. Every day, we can give birth to a new aspect of ourselves.

Every day, we can invent, understand, create something new. Every day, we can be better and, on a small scale, travel through the three antechambers of the dialectical process. Just as a new sun rises every day, we can be reborn better every day.

Exhortation or Recognition of Ignorance

Exhortation is a true clarion call for the consciousness. Socrates invents the examination of consciousness: the recognition of ignorance. A sincere self-examination allows for the recognition and acceptance of one's erroneous, rigid ideas, the pride of one's ego, the real obstacles that prevent one from moving forward on the path. This leads to the recognition of one's ignorance.

What did I believe to be true, that is false? What do I believe I do well, that I do poorly? Where do I make mistakes? For these errors stem from an ignorance that I must acknowledge to discover my shortcomings. This exhortation of consciousness enables us to illuminate erroneous areas, to clean them, to take responsibility for them, to recognize them, and understand that there is something missing within us. The recognition of ignorance leads to the love, or quest, for what we lack.

Two paths lie before us: one of not accepting our errors, ignorance, remaining pedantic, egocentric, and justifying ourselves by wanting to prove; or one of accepting what we are and deciding that something must be done to move forward.

It is the recognition of what we lack that gives birth to love. Initially, this awareness expresses itself as suffering in the face of the absence of a higher dimension for which we are nostalgic. The introspection prompted by this exhortation leads us deep within ourselves, to the Socratic discovery that we only know that we know nothing, but also to the discovery of our need to love and seek wisdom. It is this *re-cognition* that leads us out of ignorance.

This new concern leads us from ignorance to philosophy, or love of wisdom. Ignorance, according to Socrates, is not a lack of knowledge but continuing to ignore what we know that we do not know. One cannot ignore ignorance without being unable to learn. For Socrates, ignoring ignorance is the most terrible of diseases. Our true inner enemy is what pushes us to resign ourselves to ignorance with fatalism, to renounce developing a deep need for inner change, to give up any will for transformation: "I am like this! What can I do? I can't help it!" For Socrates, renouncing one's capacity for transformation is to be already dead.

Like the *black work* of the Alchemists, Socrates invites us to descend deep within ourselves and find our essential raw material, which, though submerged and covered by the dross of our doubts and fears, is the adamantine stone, the matrix of our future luminous consciousness.

Refutation or Purification of Ignorance

We must learn to purify ourselves of our ignorance because it conceals our wisdom. Just as metal is purified once the gangue surrounding it, with its mineral salts, is dissolved in the depths of the mine, we must purify ourselves of our ignorance by freeing ourselves from our prejudices, pseudo-knowledge, misunderstood ideas and finally, the sophist that inhabits us.

Purification is a path to rid ourselves of erroneous ideas, through dialogue or the ascension of consciousness. Through a precise interrogation, one "purges" oneself from intellectual and emotional errors that hide the vision of truth. This purge is also moral, leading us to not only recognize our mistakes but also feel shame for wanting to perpetuate them.

Through confrontation initiated by dialogue, we become aware of our responsibility, by confronting our doubts and fears, by accessing ever clearer and purer thoughts.

The antechamber of philosophy frees us from intellectual accumulation, allowing us to release ourselves from the superfluous and achieve ever greater clarity. Philosophy, as taught by Socrates, leads to a discipline of life which itself leads to simplicity.

The first antechamber, that of ignorance, gives birth to love; and the second leads to will, to the strength of ascension or surpassing oneself, to the practice of rigor and discipline. This ascent occurs within oneself, as well as in facing obstacles from the environment, compelling one to simplify oneself and feel increasingly lighter. This first vestibule leads from intellectual knowledge to vision, to the contemplation of things. This is what the Greeks called theory: a principle of unification that connects particular phenomena with a universal principle or law.

In alchemy, the phase of purification is called the *white work,* which allows the extraction of the metal from the gangue, to bring it to daylight from the depths of the mine.

Testing Intuition

How can we know if intuitions correspond to truth or if they are the fruit of fantasy? How can we distinguish true inspirations and intuitions, obtained in dreams or received from one's *daimon* or inner voice, from mere speculations or projections? For Socrates, the dialectical method is the tool for this test.

Indeed, if intuition is, according to the Larousse dictionary, the "immediate grasp of a truth, without the aid of reasoning", if it is a precious tool for information and inspiration, for it to become understandable, transmittable, and usable, it must pass through the sieve of reason. It is this confrontation that will test its consistency and determine if it is a mere figment of the mind, an illusion, or if on the contrary it carries authentic, new, and useful information.

When Archimedes, by making his bath overflow in Syracuse, exclaimed "Eureka" (I have found it), he had the intuition of the principle of density. But it is because he translated this intuition into a law expressed by a formula that everyone could access the understanding and use of this principle. By formulating his intuition, he validated it, and his subjective experience became objective, comprehensible, and usable by all. Similarly, a work of art is the translation, first in the mental plane and then in the sensible world, of an inspiration.

It is the role of dialectic to turn intuition into knowledge, integrated into our consciousness. It allows us to verify and translate it.

Socrates is neither an atheist nor agnostic. It is in the spiritual plane that dialectic plays a major role. For the first time, it becomes possible to translate spiritual experiences into clear terms. Dialectic exercises a double purification in the spiritual dimension. Not only does it purify illusions of fantasy and the tyranny of subjectivity, as we have seen, it also purifies religion from superstition and fanaticism (which Socrates' detractors could not tolerate).

If Socrates adopted the intellectual tool, it is primarily for greater effectiveness in the domain of concrete action, by protecting against subjectivity, impulsiveness, and passion. The dialectical method is a means, not the end that modernity has often made it out to be. Socrates does not confine the world or the individual to a method because what is crucial is the contact with the higher or divine part which is within each person. Indeed, "Socrates relies on reasoned argument to judge... yet he also feels the obligation to obey orders that reach him through supernatural means... Between these two commitments, he sees no contradiction. He posits as a principle that they are in perfect harmony."[12]

Here we encounter another type of dialogue, one that enables true inner transformation, that governs maieutics, or self-birth. It is no longer a dialogue between two people reflecting together, but an inner dialogue between an intuition, an inspiration, and an intelligence that provides a channel for it to find its fulfillment in a work, action, or object.

Maieutics or Self-Birth

The word maieutics is derived from the Greek *maieutikè*, the art of midwifery, which comes from *maia*, meaning midwife. Analogous to his mother's work, Socrates was called "the midwife of Athens" who brought hundreds of Athenian citizens into the light of the spirit. Through his interrogations, Socrates sought to extract and reveal from the souls of his interlocutors, what they knew, without knowing that they knew it. This happened with the famous Meno, who was silenced by Socrates' questions, and then gradually discovered his unconscious knowledge of the Pythagorean theorem. To discover what one knows, to know who one is, to recognize one's intrinsic value, one's Being - this is the goal of maieutics.

One cannot give birth to what one does not possess or is not. Socrates can only provide assistance, like a midwife to a woman in labor. The light that is born, the wisdom that is revealed, is not that of Socrates but belongs to the one who gives birth to himself. One cannot give to another what they do not possess. However, one can help them express what they are.

According to Socrates, through dialectic we access knowledge that we have possessed since the origin of the world, but which we have forgotten due to the impact of the soul's incarnation in matter. All true knowledge for Socrates is a reminiscence, a recalling by the soul that remembers. It is purification and the need to return to the light that gives the soul the ability to use pure thought again, to remember and express Being.

Like the third phase in the work of alchemy, *the red work*, maieutics proceeds to transform the philosopher into a sage.

Maieutics is the science of self; it makes knowledge the force that directs spiritual and concrete activity. Socratic wisdom consists of conquering oneself, while ignorance consists of being defeated by oneself. This wisdom is put into practice through virtue, which leads to true happiness or *eudaimonia*, consisting of doing good without seeking reward.

Socrates teaches us by his example that a man at peace with his conscience is wise. The wise will be able to face with calmness, the mystery of death at every moment while living fully at the same time.

CHAPTER 3

THE PATH TO HAPPINESS

The Ultimate Goal of Socrates: Happiness

For Socrates, the ultimate goal is not knowledge for its own sake, but inner happiness, or *eudaimonia*. This is his "treasure", thanks to which, he held on until the end, despite adversity and pressures of the environment; free from all excess, in an attitude of perfect balance.

Happiness - *eudaimonia* - is for Socrates the ultimate and unconditional good. "It is the only good we seek or desire for its own sake and it is, therefore, the end - *telos* - of all our actions."[1] Nothing is dearer to us. Behind the motivations for all we do, we seek happiness. It is the ultimate goal. All questioning ceases when we find it.

"There is no need to ask someone who wants to be happy: 'Why does he want to be happy?' We already have the final answer."[2] By saying that happiness is the end of all our actions, it does not mean that we think of happiness in every daily act. However, it is the ultimate reason we could give to justify our choice of any action. In other words, once happiness is given as the reason, further questioning is meaningless.

The word used by Socrates is *eudaimonia*, generally translated as happiness, but it is not just any happiness. *Eudaimonia*, which includes the word *daimon*, "allows one to reach the highest realms of intensity, at the same level as *makar*, or *makarios* indicating the capacity to access the vision of what is holy... evoking a felicity so marvelous that even the gods could not ask for anything better, and conversely, we could not ask them for a greater gift."[3] It is an inner state that allows us to share in the world of the gods.

A person in a state of *eudaimonia* is connected with their mystery: it ends all confusion and questioning. The individual is in a state of clarity, and their true identity, previously hidden, is revealed in its fullness.

Happiness is sufficient in itself. It puts an end to dialectical questioning and to any path of reason, for it moves on to another plane that does not fall within the realm of reason. Happiness indeed marks a threshold between two worlds: that of mortals, "unhappy" by nature, and that of the gods, happy by nature. Among the Greeks, this threshold was symbolized by Mount Helicon, whose summit marks the boundary between earth and sky; where also the muses reside. The ascent of Helicon follows a spiral movement, with the diameter narrowing as one draws closer to the summit.

This ascent illustrates the dialectical process, which by progressively exhausting the questioning, leads to synthesis and unity. By reaching the summit, one has integrated the law of nature (an aspect of the divine), and engages in the practice of arts and sciences, through works inspired by the Muses, as an expression of their happiness.

Why don't many people achieve happiness? Due to excessive critical reasoning. Instead of ascending, they fall into the trap of endless reasoning, leading to complaints, questions, and procrastination. Since they do not pass these through the sieve of dialectic, they fail to exhaust the resources of reason and drown in the rumination of an analytical mind left to itself. This confinement stems from an excessive identification with the personal ego or the little self, which needs to reassure itself, justify itself, and be right at all cost. Far from bringing happiness closer, the titanic effort that this requires, only drives it further away. For happiness is, by definition, universal openness.

Happiness occurs when reason, having completed its journey, falls silent. It is indeed when the complementarity of two seemingly contradictory elements, becomes irrefutably evident that happiness emerges. It is simultaneous with the vision of the totality thus perceived and with one's adherence to this totality.

Thus, light and darkness, rest and activity, when perceived in their complementarity, unite within the one who has integrated them, bringing rhythm to an otherwise difficult existence. To experience them as opposites is to reject one or the other, either constantly or alternately. This rejection inevitably causes dysfunction and unhappiness, as we often observe in ourselves and around us. Happiness is inseparable from union - with oneself, with others, and with the world around us. It takes root within us when functioning through opposition and exclusion disappears, making way for functioning through complementarity and inclusion.

But there is no happiness without exigence, which is essential for changing planes, or levels of consciousness. For Socrates, this need lies in the dialectical approach, which allows for confrontation with reality and detachment from one's emotional states.

Being: Socrates' Value System

One cannot understand Socrates' approach or method without being interested in the value system that underlies it.

Indeed, as demonstrated by Gregory Vlastos, Socrates acts according to a precise system of values.[4] For him, there are four types of good.

- The ultimate Good is happiness.
- The good that constitutes happiness is virtue.

These two categories of the higher Good - the ultimate Good being happiness and the moral good being virtues - find their source in the inner life, in being. They are not conditioned by anything external.

- Secondary goods, such as health, wealth, etc., depend on circumstances and external conditions. They pertain to *having*. They are not moral - Socrates calls them non-moral goods - but they can contribute to our happiness, if we use them wisely. While health, wealth, etc., are good and desirable, according to Socrates, they cannot fundamentally undermine the inner happiness, that is independent of them although they are not excluded. One cannot seek them at the expense of virtue. "But they are nevertheless good; we will be happier with them than without them, but only if we use them correctly, as they are not 'good by themselves'. If they are separated from wisdom, they will turn sour for us, and we will be worse off than we would have been without them."[5] These are what Socrates calls subordinate or conditional goods.

- Lastly, accessory goods, which we would call consumer goods today (house, car, computer, etc.), are neither good nor bad, as their value is purely functional. They only have value, relative to the services they can render. They do not contribute to lasting happiness because they are perishable and can be taken from us. One cannot be truly happy if one's happiness is subject to possessions or external conditions that pertain to appearance, to having and not to being. True happiness indeed cannot be lost. That is why it cannot be conditioned by having, as in reality, one cannot possess anything but oneself. Socrates insists on the necessity of self-mastery, in other words, possessing oneself, the only "possession" that can lead to happiness.

Socrates, "does not say that the non-moral goods that he spoke of (money, reputation, prestige), have no value at all, but that their value is significantly lower to that of the most precious good in life, which is the perfection of the soul... He explains why this perfection must hold such a preeminent place in our scale of values: it is what makes all other things good; without it, nothing else would be a good."[6] Possession of non-moral goods increases our happiness if and only if we possess the wisdom to correctly guide their use. No non-moral good, is good by itself. It becomes good if its use is directed by wisdom through the practice of philosophy.

The Condition of Happiness: Virtue

In the Socratic approach, virtue is not merely a means to achieve happiness. Ordinarily, once a goal is reached, the means used to achieve it are discarded, having served their purpose. In contrast, regarding virtue, while distinguishing it from happiness, Socrates reminds us that it is also constitutive of it. Consequently, they are inseparable and continuously nurture each other.

"The supreme good..., both necessary and sufficient for our happiness, is virtue... It should be the goal guiding all our actions, because... if we obtain this constituent of the good, we possess the ultimate good: we will be happy."[7] Happiness according to Socrates is not reduced to immediate interest or pleasure, although it does not exclude them. It is not egocentric. It is a happiness linked to sharing a universal good, that of virtue and wisdom. Socrates' dialectical method allows for moving from the particular to the universal, connecting the part to the whole. It thus confers the possibility of entering into contact with universal laws.

The dialectical approach opens access to the cosmos as an intelligent order, expression of the cosmic intelligence (*theos*). It prevents the individual from a purely sentimental access to the divine and makes them capable of accessing, through the channel of the mind, the plane of divine intelligence, the seat of principles and archetypes. When one becomes capable of accessing the universal and integrating into it, they can then perceive God. They then access a conscious participation in an intelligent universal order.

The practice of virtue appears as the means to develop this level of consciousness and translates it concretely into behavior, beyond purely intellectual understanding.

Virtues are universal in nature. Their practice, therefore, allows through individual behavior to achieve and express a universal dimension, and to resolve the apparent contradiction between the universal and the particular. Whenever the smallest, most anonymous of men stands up against cowardice, he embodies the virtue of courage in all its power. Likewise, a mother's unconditional devotion to her child embodies the virtue of love.

What is Virtue?

Virtue (*areté*) according to Socrates is the ability to live a certain number of principles and values in daily life. Their practice allows for leading a moral life, that is, acting in accordance with what one thinks. There is no happiness without a moral life. It is the moral life that allows us to transform our behavior and learn from our experiences, mobilizing virtues in daily life, without which happiness is not possible.

Virtue is practical application of knowledge composed of five qualities, oriented in a cross, like the four cardinal points, around a center occupied by wisdom. These are courage (*andreia*), temperance or moderation (*sophrosyne*), justice or probity (*dikaiosyne*), piety or devotion (*hosiotês*), and finally wisdom (*sophia*). This set of virtues constitutes the compass of behavior. Not using it to guide one's actions, in other words, not practicing virtue, is what causes anxiety, frustration, fear, anger, guilt, in other words, a fall in consciousness.

Why are we so often disappointed after the satisfaction of a desire? Why do we often feel so bad when, in order to gain some advantage, we have contravened a virtue, even if we have buried this failing in the unconscious? Why do we become critical and resentful of those who possess the same virtue? Because we are unable to recognize that we've stopped practicing it. Why, does confessing a wrongdoing, bring relief? Because, in doing so, we practice the virtue of acknowledging truth. This explains the need for purification. Why does injustice affect us? Because of the unjust within us. We carry injustice within us, and it is unbearable. If we can rid ourselves of it, we will no longer commit it, and it will no longer be able to affect us.

The ancients spoke of Virtue and virtues (courage, temperance, justice, devotion, wisdom). Virtue is the intrinsic quality, essential to each of us, our deepest identity. But this identity, our deep Self, does not express itself fully and immediately in our daily lives. We only perceive it in a potential state. It has to find its way through the labyrinth of our personality's characteristics. This quest of the Self, seeking its expression, explains the question we all ask ourselves: Who am I? And how can I express it? This question is the implicit recognition by each of us that we are something other than what we appear to be. It is the sign that we have left ignorance behind and taken the first step in the philosophical quest.

Virtue, or being, expresses itself in our lives through the virtues. Virtues succeed to express it, when after a long exercise, the individual has managed to make his person, the channel of his essence. Virtue, once liberated, expresses itself through concrete behavior, actions corresponding to each virtue. When virtues are not actualized, the essential virtue cannot be expressed. The Virtue of healing, if not expressed through the virtues of courage, temperance, etc., will not be able to express itself. Practicing the virtues is the way to liberate the being we truly are. This is why, better than an intellectual approach, the practice of virtues is the means of getting to know our true nature and to encounter it. The practice of virtues enables us to master ourselves: our body, our emotions and our mind. When practiced, they become the channels of expressing Virtue. They bring us the only happiness that cannot be taken away from us, that of our true being expressing itself.

The soul can be compared to music, and personality to an instrument. For the being to play music, he must first have the courage to take possession of the instrument. One has to moderate gestures to avoid damaging the instrument or producing discordant sounds. You also have to play in tune, in rhythm. Then the musician can begin to serve the music, and bring it to concrete form from the plane of potential in which it was. He can finally put his soul into it, love it and share it. The virtuoso is the one who succeeds in expressing Virtue. Self-mastery through the practice of the virtues allows one to be born to the Self.

Defect: Lack of Virtue

In reality, contrary to what we believe, virtue is natural to us. It is not the absence of virtue that causes defects, but rather the poor application of it. Each virtue is, in fact, a harmonious behavior between two extremes - of falling short by deficiency on one hand, and by excess on the other. For example, courage is situated between cowardice and temerity.

What matters is to understand that virtue is like an inner force that is difficult to apply with balance and harmony; either because of the fear of practicing virtue, clumsiness, or a sense of inadequacy. It is true that it is difficult to transition from intention into action, and this force slips away very easily. It requires a lot of skill, which implies the need for great vigilance and confidence. Until one masters the force of virtue, one slips into the rut of defect, either through excess or deficiency. Hence it is said that one has the defects of one's qualities. A defect is merely the shadow of the soul's qualities - a lack of virtue. Recognizing one's defects and accepting them is the best way to identify the virtues one potentially possesses. Defects are the raw material, akin to the lead of the alchemists that transmutes into gold, into virtues, through the philosophical approach.

When this force is channeled along the path of the golden mean - between excess and deficiency - the initial defect transforms into a virtue. One then reaches the plane of inner bliss, *eudaimonia*, the divine plane of irreversible attainments. To transition from a state where the material is still undifferentiated, to one where deep qualities are expressed, the philosopher must accept transformation. In other words, he must accept a change of form, expressed as a new attitude towards his defects. He decides to stop being an instrument of the defects; he accepts and then transcends them. He no longer uses them as a means to an end, for the end does not justify the means. Instead, he establishes a framework that enables the personality to manifest the soul's qualities objectively, and express inner life.

Just as courage, as mentioned earlier, lies between the two extremes of cowardice and temerity, temperance lies between apathy (in the literal sense of insensitivity) and excessive asceticism, or apathy and debauchery; justice between subjectivism and fanaticism; piety between egoism and superstition; wisdom between ignorance and intellectualism.

As we have just seen, defects rise when there are shortcomings in the daily application of virtues. Observing our own clumsiness and deficiencies helps us become aware of the virtues struggling to express themselves within us. This is why, for Socrates, evil does not exist in itself; it is ignorance, i.e. lack of skill in expressing virtues, that translates into evil.

Understanding the true nature of happiness is therefore fundamental. Living virtue is the condition for happiness.

The practice of one virtue leads to the development of others. Having one, inevitably means having them all. Thus, with the courage to temper one's excesses, one acquires temperance; this fosters a certain wisdom that opens one to devotion or piety.

Today, piety is confined to the religious domain. For Socrates, it is expressed in the phrase from *Euthyphro*: "You are him." In other words, piety is the higher feeling that allows one to become aware of, and enliven, the bonds that unite us to everything around us. Towards our parents, it expresses as filial love; towards a close one, as friendship or tenderness; in relation to religion, it expresses as devotion; and towards nature, as an ecological sentiment. Piety is the source of the sentiment of responsibility. It makes us aware of what we owe to our loved ones, to our country, to humanity, to the gods, and to nature. Piety is a feeling that entails an awareness of our duties towards other beings and things, and the free and willing acceptance to fulfilling them, because it is just.

This helps us understand the Latin definition of virtue (*virtus*). The Greek *aretê* later becomes the Latin *virtus*, a constant disposition that leads one to do good and avoid evil. We can therefore understand why Socrates insisted on the practice of virtue as a rule. The law of action was the practice of virtue for the life he had chosen. It is in fulfilling what he imposes on himself, not in submitting to desire, that he finds happiness, a voluntary happiness. As a moral obligation, he accepts the price that comes with it. "I would rather fail by acting nobly than win by acting vile." This declaration by Neoptolemus in Sophocles' *Philoctetes* could very well have been made by Socrates. Such is the moral life.

In other philosophical schools in the classical (ancient) manner, this practice is also called discipleship: the sharing of inner teachings through lived experience. It is the ability to implement this practice by oneself and for oneself; to exit from the system of external constraints in order to adhere to inner necessities or obligations.

A Socrates Close to the Orientals

Socrates understands reality, dispels its illusions, focuses on the essential rather than the accessories to achieve a stable and permanent state that allows him to always be happier, and never less. His guiding principle is to be happy. He attains bliss, or enlightenment as a Buddhist would say. He unites with this state, which is the supreme good. His happiness does not come from any external good or event, but from an internal state and choice, which for him is always the best choice. He accepts a number of rules he imposes on himself. If he can have an accessory good that amplifies happiness, he would take it; if not, however, it is not a problem. He has no qualms, never has anything to lose, and never stops being in contact with the world, people, and things.

In hindsight, this is an oriental attitude, which is closer to a state of emptiness, the source of fullness, than to the happiness that resides in possession for a Westerner. When Socrates says he has nothing to give, it is because he cannot offer anything more than himself. He has no possessions since he has *chosen to be* rather *than to have*. This is what constitutes his fullness. This is also disconcerting, and in this sense, he is close to Zen. He may not answer a question for weeks or years, waiting for the disciple to find the answer himself. However, he is capable of repeating the same thing a thousand times, to bring the disciple back to the need to find the answer.

Exercising sovereignty, the power one has over oneself, is the exercise of virtue. The choice lies on the ethical plane but corresponds to a universal law, which the Hindus call *dharma,* which invites detachment. May our actions always be in harmony with the universal law, the one that moves the world. Free from all impulsiveness, may we remain on the middle path, the path of harmony, without causing any imbalance, without collateral effects corresponding to the notion of karma in Hindu philosophy. A musician, who is master of his instrument and is attentive to the gestures of the conductor, will not make a false note that disrupts the harmony of the whole. In this, Socrates joins the Orientals.

When he says, for example, that it is better to suffer injustice than to commit it, Socrates is happy, he does not suffer. He transcends the source of pain, sorrow, sadness. He practices detachment. Injustice has no hold on him and cannot cause him to deviate from virtue, nor alter his inner happiness. He is a philosopher in the classical manner, free from attachment and desire.

The path of Socrates is an existential path of action; it is not intellectual. The moral philosopher has an existential practice to achieve happiness. Socrates does not submit to the temptation of the law of retaliation. This does not correspond with a Western attitude. He does not call for vengeance, he does not hate, he does not demand reparation, he is not vindictive. He nips in the bud the spirit of revenge of the personal ego, that he transcends. He becomes transpersonal and settles into the Self. He becomes universal.

CHAPTER 4

SOCRATIC PEDAGOGY: IRONY

The wisdom of Socrates is put into action through virtue. It leads to happiness - *eudaimonia* - which is the happiness of the wise, of working well, of being good. This happiness generates true love, giving without seeking reward. It is an active wisdom that cannot be transmitted.

Indeed, all this leads us to the limits of what can be conveyed through language or dialogue. For example, how can one understand justice without practicing it? Socrates has knowledge to share, but which he cannot transmit. The individual decision to put this knowledge into practice, is imperative for it to emerge from within oneself, because it can be acquired only from within.

While an intellectual framework, a line of research, can be transmitted, there is a certain universal timeless knowledge that is not transmittable. In order to appropriate an idea and make it more than something said by someone, regardless of the authority of the other, it is essential to rediscover it within oneself. Knowledge cannot be shared as long as one merely repeats it without having experienced it for ourselves, without having chosen it ourselves for ourselves. Endlessly, each of us is called to rediscover what others have discovered.

The true master-disciple relationship is established only when the disciple rediscovers within himself what the master has said. Until the disciple has made it his own, no progress is possible. The master can only provide the framework. He knows that his role is to prepare, to open the way for such a process. That is why, the method always involves questioning the individual himself: Will he resolve to live consciously according to what he has understood? "Direct language is powerless to communicate the experience of existence, the authentic consciousness of being, the seriousness of lived experience, the solitude of decision."[1] Maieutics is the affair of each person. That is why, as Cicero said, "The discussion practiced by Socrates was to refute other reasonings while affirming nothing himself."

Socrates uses irony not to mock people or hide anything, but because irony is the only rhetorical and pedagogical construct that, on the one hand, allows the awakening of the disciple, and on the other hand, pushes him to find answers within himself. "Socratic irony expresses the tension between ignorance (i.e. the impossibility to express with words) and the direct experience of the unknown, i.e. the existence of the just man, whose justice reaches the divine level."[2]

The challenge is to move from the darkness of ignorance, which is the absence of truth, to the darkness of the unknown, which hides a truth. The interlocutor, by purifying himself of ignorance, brings forth a transcendent truth or wisdom within himself. The function of irony is to facilitate this passage.

The Mask of Socrates

Through irony, Socrates discovers the shadow of the other - reminiscent of C. G. Jung - and brings it to light. He creates a projection of the interlocutor's self. He reveals what the other does not want to see in himself: this is the mask of Socrates. He acts as a mirror, reflecting to the other his own image, his questions, his defects, and his nature, to the point that dealing with him is uncomfortable. Socrates does not reveal himself because his objective is to free the other. When the other drops his own mask, when he no longer shields himself, Socrates' mask also falls, and one meets the true Socrates.

The interlocutor, in turn, projects his problem onto Socrates until he realizes that all this concerns him. When he realizes he is facing his own image, he becomes aware of his ignorance. Socrates operates indirectly, through metaphor, symbol, analogy, and image. He forces his interlocutor to use his creative, symbolic imagination. "It is about making the reader aware of his error, not by directly refuting it, but by exposing it in such a way that its absurdity becomes clear to him."[3] This evokes what Nietzsche said on pedagogy: "An educator never says what he thinks, but always and only how he thinks something will be useful for the one he is educating."[4]

Socratic irony is a loving irony. It employs the technique of reversal. Socrates is interested in someone, asks questions, out of love. The other, puzzled, wonders what is happening, and his first reaction is a form of rejection. But, paradoxically, at a certain point in the dialogue and self-questioning, touched by what Socrates says, he becomes interested. The lover has made the other fall in love. This is the moment when Socrates chooses to disengage from his interlocuter, so the latter turns his interest towards himself and comes to find the answer within himself, and not in Socrates. He then shares with Socrates the truth, and the happiness of having found it.

Socrates knows he cannot transmit anything but can awaken the other to the knowledge buried within him. He awakens his interlocutor so that the latter comes to desire that Socrates communicate to him his wisdom or knowledge. But Socrates leads him far beyond that: he brings him to find wisdom within himself, even if it means passing through moments of despair.

Socrates masks himself; in other words, he plays a role, like an actor in the Greek theater who wears the mask of a character. In Socrates' case, this mask is that of his interlocutor. When the latter recognizes it as such, he frees himself from it and can truly be himself. The reversal that occurs following the dialectical exchange is extraordinary. By removing his own mask, in fact, the disciple accesses the hidden dimension of Socrates and contemplates his inner beauty, or even that of the god who dwells within him. This is how Alcibiades' comparison is understood, when he likens Socrates to the

Silenus-shaped cases that served as caskets for the statuettes of the gods.

We sometimes hold ourselves in such high regard, that we place ourselves on a level that prevents us from seeking wisdom and knowledge. Socrates feigns ignorance, acts naive, places himself below his interlocutor's level so that the latter understands his true level. To make him realize his egocentrism, see how much he overestimated himself, and become aware of his ignorance. The roles then reverse: the interlocutor finds himself in the position that truly corresponds to him, that of ignorance. This is the moment when irony leads to disturbance, comparable to the turmoil of love. It can result in resentment and rejection. Or, conversely, the realization caused by the disturbance gives rise to the humility necessary to advance and leads to the philosophical conversion that constitutes the first step of the Socratic method.

By highlighting it, Socrates makes it possible to bring something that was buried, into the light within the other. If the latter accepts it when he sees it, he is then rid of it and finds a new confidence, no longer in his superiority, but in the existence of truth and his own ability to discover it; in his inner master rather than an external one.

The game of irony played by Socrates' mask is essential for one to be able to appropriate the truth, because this appropriation rarely occurs in a direct manner. It is utopian to believe that simply saying things is enough to integrate them. "I don't understand, I had warned him, he knew!" is an often heard lament. It is not only about unveiling the truth, but also to know how to present it in a form that gives the other the courage to do what is needed to appropriate it. Assimilation is a complex process. And if the pedagogy of truth were not such a subtle art, there would be many like Socrates!

The Shock of Irony

Irony - *eironeia* - appears among the Greeks as a psychological attitude in which the individual seeks to appear inferior than he is, to pass for an ordinary or even superficial person, to pretend to agree with his interlocutor. In reality, because he has no negative intention, Socrates transforms usual irony. His irony is not about deception, hypocrisy, or malice: it aims to convey understanding. It causes a shock, a questioning. It makes the interlocutor think about something he had not considered before.

As demonstrated by Gregory Vlastos, Socrates reverses the rhetorical formula of irony into a figure of speech that Quintilian would formulate several centuries later, by Latinizing irony – *ironia*; a figure of speech whereby "the opposite of what is said must be understood." Webster reiterates in the 18th century, "irony consists of using words to express something other than its literal meaning, especially its opposite." Irony is a means to handle contradictions.

"Socrates splits himself: there is on one side the Socrates who knows in advance how the discussion will end, but there is also the other Socrates who will make the entire dialectical journey with his interlocutor. The latter does not know where Socrates is leading him. This is the irony."[5]

The method is as follows:

1. He takes his interlocutor's position as a starting point.
2. He gradually makes him admit all the consequences of this position.
3. He constantly seeks his agreement, obtained by subjecting him to rational demands. By linking together the agreements obtained, he demonstrates the contradiction contained in the starting position.

At this point, the interlocutor realizes that he does not really know why he acts the way he does. Even if he has understood nothing, the important thing is that Socrates' guidance has led him to experience the activity of the mind: the consciousness.

Complex Irony

Unlike the sophists who use simple irony, where the signified does not correspond to what is said, Socrates uses "complex" irony. "What is said corresponds and at the same time does not correspond to what is signified. The apparent content must be understood as true in one sense and false in another."[6] This allows Socrates to handle the apparent contradictions present in reality, which for him is both true and false at once. Irony requires an effort of understanding and interpretation from the listener.

Socrates transforms irony in the usual sense, by removing the lack of sincerity from it. "The fact that Socrates claims to teach nothing... If one considers the banal sense of the word, 'teaching' refers to the mere transfer of knowledge from the teacher's mind to the student's, and in this case, Socrates means what he says: he does not practice this kind of teaching. But, in the sense he would like to give to 'teaching,' the word refers to the process of engaging candidates for learning in refutative discussion, making them aware of their ignorance and then capable of discovering the truth by themselves, which the teacher did not want to reveal. In this sense of the word, Socrates would readily admit that he teaches, that he is even the only true teacher. When he engages in dialogue with his disciples, the intended effect - which is indeed obtained - is to stimulate and support their effort of moral improvement."[7]

Through this path of teaching, which is irony, Socrates is not a guru but a companion, associated with the quest of the other. Those who accuse him of deception, have not, in reality, been deceived by what he said, but by the way they interpreted his words. Alcibiades is the clearest example: he believed Socrates physically loved him, for the beauty of his body, while Socrates loved his soul.

"It is possible to understand Socratic eros as a kind of complex irony comparable to that attributed to him by Alcibiades... when he says that he (Socrates) 'ignores everything and knows nothing.' By claiming he knows nothing, Socrates means, and at the same time does not mean what he says; likewise, by talking about his erotic attraction to beautiful young people, he means and does not mean what he says... In the banal sense of pederastic love, Socrates feels no love for Alcibiades or any of the young boys he pursues. And yet, he loves them, in the sense that the verb love (*eran*) can take in the theoretical and practical context of Socratic eros: their physical beauty adds a particular flavor to the affectionate interaction he has with their minds... Yes, Alcibiades was indeed deceived, otherwise he would not have devised this delusional plan (wanting to sleep with Socrates unsuccessfully). He would not have persisted so long in offering his charms to obtain wisdom while Socrates steadfastly refused to take the bait. Yes, he was deceived, but by whom? Not by Socrates, but by himself. He believed what he believed because he wanted to believe it. When Socrates says 'no' to his offer, he does so with the vigor of a Zen master striking a disciple with a stick for asking a foolish question."[8] Knowing what his disciple had in mind, he let it happen so that Alcibiades could discover the truth by himself... Socrates always leaves one the choice, even if it leads to error. Even if it causes suffering, because his main concern is related to the ultimate goal, which is for each to access the truth, and it can only be achieved by oneself, for oneself. Even if it disappoints desires, even if it causes the departure of those whose pride cannot bear the prospect of having made a mistake.

The ambiguity of complex irony, which forces one to find the meaning, liberates one from rational reasoning. It opens up space and allows for free will and self-determination. It enables intuitions and higher feelings to exercise their fertilizing power; for life to infiltrate the path of transformation. Far from any form of regimentation, it opens an ever-widening field. Socrates seeks the moral autonomy of each person. His wisdom means nothing to those who cannot live it for themselves, for only autonomy guarantees living knowledge.

CHAPTER 5

LOVE ACCORDING TO SOCRATES

Diotima, priestess of Apollo Epicurius in the Temple of Bassae, in the heart of old Arcadia, is said to have initiated Socrates into the mysteries of love in its highest form.

Love: A Lack Full of Resources

Plato reminds us that love is an expression of a lacking. Hence, we discover that to achieve bliss, or *eudaimonia*, we lack true love. Indeed, selfishness, calculation, anxiety, etc., symptoms of excessive egocentrism, highlight this lack of love. Once we become aware of it, and by falling in love with love itself, we seek to eliminate this lacking. This translates into a need for inner beauty, for harmony, best represented by Apollo, among the Greek gods.

All ancient philosophers agreed that the quest for love begins with the body and then rises to access inner beauty. "The Neoplatonist Plotinus indicates that the dialectical path towards illumination begins with sensible beauty and ascends to the plane of intelligence. In three synthetic phases, he recalls the process of the lover who loves beautiful bodies, the musician who loves beautiful sounds, and the philosopher who encounters beauty in ideas."[1]

According to Diotima, Eros is a *daimon*, an intermediate being, like Hermes, a messenger between gods and human beings, that enables them to enter into a relationship. Eros is like a clarion call, an invitation and a reminder, a possibility that opens up. He is neither wisdom nor beauty itself. According to Diotima, Love is not the love of Aphrodite, who presides over procreation; it is not sensual love as is commonly understood. Love as she conceives it, has Penia and Poros as parents. Penia, the lacking, is its mother, and its father is Poros, the inventive and cunning spirit, never short of expedients. Love is therefore a lacking that is full of resources, in perpetual back-and-forth between the two. When a desire is excessive, it is because resources are lost, and Love knows only the lacking in which it is trapped. Conversely, when sheltered in comfort, it becomes a prisoner of its resources, indolence sets in, and the lacking withers away.

However, when the two aspects combine - one related to Mars, the other to Mercury - love becomes the force that enables the opposites to connect. "The lover stands guard at the beloved's door (this is his martial side), spending the night under the stars. He is both a beggar and a soldier. But also, he is fertile in inventions (his mercurial side), a sorcerer, magician, skilled speaker, because Love makes one ingenious. For him, discouragement and hope, need and satiation, follow one another unceasingly with the successes and failures of his love."[2] In this sense, it is a hunting Eros, the prototype of Socrates, a philosopher in love who stalks his prey, and lures it into his trap, until he captures it. Unlike a hunter, however, Socrates seizes his prey only to set it free. In Plato's Symposium, Diotima reveals the significance of Eros of Socrates: "He lays traps for noble souls, for he is bold, impudent, enduring. He is a dangerous hunter, always finding some trick, eager to be clever (wise), resourceful, continually meditating some stratagem, a terrible sorcerer, magician, and sophist."[3]

"As for the robustness of Eros, it is found in the portrait of Socrates while he was in the army, as described by Alcibiades: he resists cold, hunger, fear, while being able to withstand wine as well as prolonged meditation."[4]

Socrates' Eros is love and wisdom, full of energy and life. Thus, after the five-month siege of Potidaea in Chalcidice, Alcibiades observes that Socrates, then about forty years old, quietly rises at dawn and leaves the tent. When he has moved a little away, he stops and contemplates the sunrise. The contemplation of the rising sun allows him to establish mental silence and deep concentration, causing an energy to rise within him that pierces the shell of his body, leading him out of ordinary consciousness, to contact the origins. At lunch, Socrates' place is empty. He is still standing, motionless, before the horizon, enveloped in light. It is only at dawn on the following day, that he emerges from his ecstatic state and his soul reintegrates into his body. He then finishes his prayer to Apollo, which was left unfinished, and returns to camp.[5]

The practice of Eros appears as a principle of unification that reconciles the diurnal and nocturnal aspects of existence, Apollo and Dionysus, the forces of self-mastery and regeneration. Through his method, Socrates activates the knowledge of the essential dimension in each person, applying the Apollonian mastery through struggle and effort, which gives access to the celestial world. This ascent can only be made because thought achieves harmony with the whole. By diving into himself, Socrates found the necessary strength to rise and maintain the level he reached.

Perhaps the main lacking unconsciously felt by the soul is the nostalgia of its origins, experienced as an irrepressible need for rejuvenation. This is probably what inspired Plato's Theory of Reminiscence. For him, as Delia Steinberg Guzmán explains, "Man enters the philosophical path through reminiscence, through nostalgia, through the sadness of something he once had, which he knows of intuitively, but that was lost and which he feels belongs to him." It is something he once possessed and still intuitively feels deep within himself, unable to express it... "Man becomes a philosopher when he awakens from within."[6]

The Eros of Socrates

The Eros of Socrates contradicts the theogony of Hesiod, which constitutes the foundation of Greek mythology. For Hesiod, Eros stands for the principle of generation through coupling. In fact, Socrates' concept of Eros recalls the rhapsodic theogonies of Orpheus. Orpheus spoke of a primordial Eros, "which is, so to speak, put in parentheses by Hesiod. Under the name Protogonos (First-Born) or Phanes (The One Who Shines) - in other words, one who confers the qualities in order to shine - Eros, in Orphic thought, is the force that integrates and reconciles opposites and contraries. It is the primordial force that unifies differentiated aspects in a world torn by tension."[7]

Orphic Eros is the principle that maintains the coherence of the Universe, allowing black and white, day and night to coexist. It embraces the seemingly contradictory aspect of existence. This ancient tradition, consciously or otherwise, inspires Socrates. And his convergence with Orphic thought leads him to detach from the beliefs of his fellow citizens who were strongly influenced by Hesiod's thought. "For Hesiod, only the gods matter, their respective domains, their history, which forms the true discourse on Being. And the division between gods and human beings caused by Prometheus only consecrates the order defined by divine powers."[8] In other words, the chance that the gods would truly care for human beings is slim. The world of the gods and that of human beings are two nearly parallel worlds. This explains the fatalism of Greek tragedy; the hero's tragic death as a victim of fate. The two systems reserve a very different place for man, and Socrates aligns to the idea of death as a victory over fate.

"In Orphic thought, on the contrary, anthropology is an essential chapter: it aims to explain both how the first humans appeared in an originally perfect world, how they fell into individual existence, and how they still carry within themselves a spark of divine origin."[9]

The divine spark, which according to Orphic myth, is in every human being, is a fragment of Dionysus. Dionysus was dismembered and eaten by the Titans, who represent the instinctive nature of the human being. The ashes of the Titans and the incorruptible Dionysian fragments comprise the source of the substance from which Zeus created the human being. Thus, the human being has a dual origin: the Titans and Dionysus. Consequently, he possesses hubris or excess, as well as a violent spirit, owed to the Titans. At the same time, due to his divine Dionysian origin, he has the possibility of achieving rigorous asceticism that allows him to purify himself and free himself from the prison of the body, inside which the soul is confined due to the ineptness in practicing virtue. The Orphic theory of the soul's imprisonment is one of the essential points of Socratic discourse. That is the foundation of the trust that Socrates has in the human being, despite his violent and passionate nature.

The Religion of Mysteries

The Greeks knew two types of religious life. The collective, social religion was related to the cult of each city's protective deity. Thus, in Athens, Athena had a temple atop the Acropolis, a place to connect with the divinity. She regulated the city's social and political life.

On the other hand, there was the religion of mysteries, where individual mysticism could find expression. It delivered teachings of the hidden or invisible aspect of existence, including death. The understanding of these teachings was acquired through asceticism and experience, opening access to a reality beyond reason.

There is a divine figure whose presence is constant across the various forms of mystery religions, such as Orphism and the Eleusinian Mysteries, and in mystery philosophies, such as Pythagoreanism: Dionysus. In this regard, he is not the god of wine, as in popular religion, but the power of regeneration, resurrection, victory over death and the unknown, the quintessential image of the *myste* (a candidate to be initiated into the Mysteries).

Another figure who is constantly present is Apollo. Paradoxically, prophets like Orpheus, Pythagoras, and others, present themselves as children of Apollo, the god of light, measure, harmony, balance. By assuming the telluric forces of the underworld, Apollo acquires and bequeaths the aptitude for prophecy, as to the Pythia at Delphi.

This strange pair of opposites formed by Apollo and Dionysus appears as the true ideal of the Greek world, not just limited to the city and social life, but also including the marginal practices related to the notion of initiation.

Although Socrates frequents all strata of society, he always remains on the margins. Through his presence in the city, he is the representative of this other current. He is certainly not the only one, but unlike others he shows and expresses his difference and tries to bring others to accept theirs. This is probably why he was condemned. His approach paradoxically questioned the city itself. Some oppose Dionysian and Apollonian mysticism, but in this case and in another reading, they are complementary.

Apollo is associated with the singing swan. In all traditions, the swan's song is associated with the birth or end of the world. This bird has a soaring and majestic flight like that of the spirit, a circular path recalling the primordial form of the circle, and its song pierces the dawn sky to let light through. This song is also associated with the flapping of wings: the swan makes music by playing in the air; its instrument is the sky. It therefore represents the mastery of celestial navigation. Very early on, Apollo, the god of light, integrates into the older figure of Helios, the god of the sun, and they are subsequently confused. Furthermore, the wild swan is a migratory bird. Apollo exists in the collective unconscious of the people of the time as a bridge between the North and the South. It is a reminder of the origin of all those who migrated from the North to the South towards the Mediterranean, and of their encounter with indigenous peoples. When the swan departs and returns, it is as if it goes off to seek new knowledge in the distant Hyperborea.

According to legend, in this distant land lived "a holy people, dedicated to Apollo, all of whom had a just conduct, abstained from lust, knew neither disease nor old age, delighted in music and dance."[10] They were bearers of primordial knowledge. This better captures the significance of this god of light, harmony, and beauty. He is a virile adolescent with feminine features, as god of music and poetry, and who would acquire the gifts of healing and prophecy as per the shamanic techniques of ecstasy. Paradoxically, the prophets of the Apollonian lineage, of whom Orpheus is the most illustrious, exhibit a shamanic profile.

The shaman Dionysus, complementary to Apollo, travels to the East. He passes through Egypt and India. Together, they form the cross of the four cardinal points, the union of opposites.

In his measured, serene, rational expression, Socrates is Apollonian. In his constant regenerative capacity, his peculiar sense of humor, his inspired nature, his ecstatic experiences, his mastery over intoxication, he expresses Dionysian forces. Socrates achieves a balance between the two forces which represented antipodes in the Greek world, and were symbolized by Apollo and Dionysus, respectively.

Both are present in the temple of Delphi, which played an important role in Socrates' life. One of its pediments, which bears the inscription, "Know Thyself," is dedicated to Apollo; the second, at the back of the temple, was dedicated to Dionysus. When Apollo, master of the day, of summer, of diurnal activity, retired at the end of autumn to the Hyperboreans, he was replaced by Dionysus, master of winter, of night, and nocturnal inspiration. Socrates is the expression of an ancient ideal that survives behind the popular religion and other Greek institutions.

Because it is at the center of the contradictory tension of existence, signified by Apollo and Dionysus, the temple of

Delphi houses the *omphalos*, the stone indicating the world's center, the crossroads of all routes, where heaven and earth can meet, and where therefore, oracles can be delivered, like the one that profoundly impacted the life of Socrates.

The Orphic Tradition

The Orphic tradition consists of the teachings of the Mysteries. It aims to remove violence from the human being by channeling the strength of the individual, by combating savagery in all its forms, and transforming and transcending the primitive character of the sorcerer. That is why it is so important and its imprint is so strong, though it always remains on the fringe.

Traces of the Orphic tradition (whether Orpheus is a fictional character or not) are found from the 7th century BCE. Perhaps it is older, however, as Orpheus is supposed to represent a current of wisdom that came from Egypt to lead the Greeks out of savagery to civilize them.

This tradition names Calliope, the first of the nine Muses, as his mother and the god Apollo as his father. According to other traditions, he is the son of Oeagrus, king of Thrace and who was also a river god related to Apollo. Aeschylus speaks of Orpheus as a fervent disciple of Helios, rising every morning to climb Mount Pangea and contemplate the rising of the god. "The magical powers of Orpheus manifested through singing and music (the voice), and he played a lyre, like Apollo. The instrument offered to him by the god, initially had seven strings (the lyre that Hermes had given to Apollo.) He added two more, in homage to the nine Muses,"[11] that is to say, to the nine digits of a decade which represents creation in its entirety. The lyre contains the laws of the universe, which explains its miraculous powers. It could move rocks, summon animals. Its fundamental power was to give life and consciousness to inanimate objects.

This is also what Socrates will do in his own way: his voice is his consciousness; his lyre is the dialectic and irony. Like Orpheus, he instills consciousness. What Orpheus does for nature, Socrates does for the human being.

Orpheus is also linked to Dionysus. According to Diodorus of Sicily, his paternal grandfather was Charops, a native of Thrace. As Charops had revealed to Dionysus a plot that had been hatched against him. The god initiated Charops into the mysteries of his cult and gave him a kingdom, which was later inherited by Charops' son, Oeagrus. Later, Orpheus was himself initiated into these mysteries by his father. But "being an exceptional person on account of his education and natural gifts, he made many modifications to the rites, and for this reason, the initiations originating from Dionysus (death/resurrection) were later called Orphic."[12] "As a devotee of Dionysus-Zagreus, Orpheus knew the routes to the beyond. Like all shamans, he could thwart traps and avoid the immense perils of the descent into Hell."[13]

As Yves Dacosta puts it, Orpheus is Apollo's prophet and Dionysus' disciple. "Orphism was essentially esoteric and ascetic."[14] Self-mastery allowed for initiation and it freed the imprisoned soul. The Orphic doctrine includes the belief in reincarnation, as it was in the doctrines of Pythagoras and Plato. Tablets found in tombs attest to the existence of a kind of "Orphic Book of the Dead". One passage emphasizes the importance of not wasting time in the beyond, and the need to quickly drink the fresh water from the lake of memory to recover one's roots and answer the question posed by the celestial tribunal: "Who are you? Where do you come from? - I am a son of the Earth and the Starry Heaven." In the beyond, the celestial tribunal asks the dead the quintessential philosophical question, the very same one that Socrates poses to the living: "Who are you?"

This brings to mind Plato's doctrine of reminiscence, which states that we have knowledge within us, but must remember it. Why? Because, according to the Orphic theory, we were present at the origin of world, since as seen above, we carry within us a fragment of Dionysus. If we liberate our Dionysian essence, we regain the memory of the world's origin. Plato reiterates this in his famous phrase: "Man is a god, but he has forgotten it." Even if Plato mocks the superstition of the Orphic priests of his time, his writings testify to Orphic knowledge.

A Good God, a God of Love

Orpheus' god is a good god who wants man to recover his divine nature and become a conscious participant in the cosmos again. Similarly, Socrates rejects the law of retaliation, and his god, like that of the pre-Socratics, is an impersonal being, not outside of Nature, but within it. It is a cosmic intelligence - *theos* - that accounts for the intelligible order of the universe - *cosmos*.

As a moral philosopher, Socrates does not dwell on metaphysical and cosmological considerations. However, as Gregory Vlastos states, “he could demand from his gods that they meet ethical criteria... Ionian philosophy had rationalized divinity by making it natural. From the same supernatural framework that they reject, Socrates makes an analogous shift. He rationalizes the gods by making them moral.”[15] In other words, the gods are also subject to the law of justice, or intelligent order. Hence, they cannot do as they please. “These gods can be both supernatural and rational, as long as they are rationally moral,” i.e. they do Good. Socrates develops a moral theology, contrary to the popular vision of his time, but entirely in line with the Orphic spirit. “By questioning the concept of god just enough to align it with his moral ideas, and by deriving from his new conception of the goodness of the human being, the standards to which the gods themselves are bound.”[16]

Socrates asks in *The Republic*: “Is divinity not truly good? And is this not how we must describe it? Consequently, divinity cannot be the cause of all things, but only of what is good; it is not the cause of evils.”[17] For Socrates, as for Heraclitus, divinity transcends the duality of good and evil.

When explaining the essence of piety in *Euthyphro*, Socrates specifies that it does not depend on what the gods want or do. “Piety, like each of the other virtues, has its own essence, as normative for the gods as it is for us; this essence determines what virtue is, as rigorously in their case, as in ours. (This is reminiscent of the Egyptian concept of Ma’at.) Therefore, for Socrates, just as the knowledge of good and evil leads to moral goodness in a human being, the same knowledge would lead to the same goodness in the case of a god. And since the deity's wisdom surpasses that of even the wisest human, its goodness must also surpass equally immensely that of the most virtuous man."[18]

Socrates proposes human wisdom, in the service of a good God. This leads to his particular conception of piety, since this is how he can be of service to both the human being and to God. His rite is sharing and awakening. "Piety consists in doing the work of a god for the benefit of human beings."[19] This is the revolution of Socratic piety, subversive for the Greeks of the time. For him, the human being is a channel of divinity, of his own divinity, and of cosmic intelligence. It is not through sacrifice or prayer that one can enter into a relationship with God, but through the divinity within oneself. It is this fragment of the cosmic being that connects to God.

"A man practicing Socratic piety would not, in his prayer to the deity ask: 'Let my will be done by you' but rather, 'Let your will be done by me'... (The gods) want nothing for humans, except what they themselves would want, if their will were wholly oriented towards the good."[20] Such a man renounces selfish happiness to become a channel for divine will. His actions, having become transpersonal, he finds true happiness.

CONCLUSION: REBORN THROUGH HAPPINESS

If we do not achieve a certain inner happiness, everything we do in life is pointless. What matters is the acquisition of goods that no one can take from us. Astonishingly, despite the twenty-five centuries that have passed, this proposition of Socrates is still entirely relevant.

Our disappointment with the resounding failure of ideologies and mass solutions attempted in the 20th century has led to several observations. We must return to the individual, capable of harmonious relationships with society and nature. One cannot make people happy without their participation, let alone the case that it is against their will. No progress is possible without each person taking responsibility for themselves. Rather than accumulating knowledge, it is crucial to learn how to learn. We must open ourselves up, question ourselves, and rather than remain on an intellectual plane, translate ideas into concrete actions.

The image of Socrates subtly looms in the background of today's needs and the insights gained from our experiences.

In the era of Socrates, everything was being invented. Philosophical concepts and ideas, which remain with us today after so many centuries, had the vigor and brilliance of the new. They were bearers of hope.

Today, words have been exhausted, because they have gradually become empty of their meaning. We can do without words, but we cannot live without meaning. We are so afraid to use certain words, to name things, that our imprisoned souls can no longer express themselves, and we have prematurely aged. We fear courage because the word is overused, piety because it sounds sanctimonious, temperance because it seems uptight. We fear justice because it sounds demagogic, and we fear wisdom because it seems naive.

Let us restore meaning to words, relearn them, and make them alive in our daily lives through our own example.

Let us accept to be reborn, to give birth to Virtue from the depths of ourselves, for that is the quality of our Being. Socrates showed us that this is possible and that it is the result of a two-stage journey; we can avoid neither the journey, nor the obstacles it is strewn with. The ascent serves to rid ourselves of ignorance; it drives the dispossession and purification that is inherent in catharsis, enabling the control and overcoming of passions that alienate us. The descent, or return to daily life, allows us to confront our intuitions and discoveries with reality and validate them. "The exercise of pure thought, purified from bodily or passionate constraints, undoubtedly represents, the core of philosophical activity for Socrates."[1]

The benefit of this ascent-and-return is rebirth, a reconciliation with oneself that allows us to share an inner state of happiness that no external circumstance can take away, a permanent source of comfort and inspiration in existence.

Inner happiness cannot be transmitted. We cannot give it to others, but we can share it. *Eudaimonia* is a state of enthusiasm. It is a radiating force that can encourage others to begin the quest. The quest for happiness requires courage, and courage allows us to start off.

Encouraged by examples, we can muster up our own courage. The observation of nature is one source of encouragement - its magnificence, strength, happiness, and the enthusiasm it radiates. There are also human sources of encouragement. Despite power struggles, injustice, and lies, and even if the forces of evil often triumph, there are always artists who capture beauty, thinkers who grasp knowledge, people who fight oppression and ignorance. These pearls, intact amidst mediocrity and chaos, are also an encouragement to recognize the fleeting brilliance of this divine dimension that human beings can share in, with the gods.

There is no happiness without love. Happiness is impossible without the bond of Eros created between things, the unifying love. He transforms opposition, antagonism, and war into harmony and balance.

Happiness is a state of union in which we are one with ourselves, with others, and with nature; a state of resonance, in a relationship that transcends intellect and words. Happiness gives birth to the true individual because it allows one to express their identity, not in opposition to others, but in relation to them. The energy of happiness is powerfully transformative. When we experience happiness, everything else - circumstances or states of mind - becomes trivial and insignificant. The state of happiness brings together the fragments that make up who we are. Consequently, it allows us to attain unity. When we lack happiness, we long for it and find ourselves in a state of malaise.

Losing happiness is to lose touch with oneself, to no longer belong to oneself; it is to be "out of it", as the saying goes. It is not to know who we are, to make unintended gestures, and to utter words we did not intend to say. It is to become a stranger to oneself, to the point that inner dialogue is disrupted and silenced. We experience unhappiness when we are disconnected from ourselves, when we stray from the channels built and constituted by the practice of virtues. These channels are the path to express the deeper self. One who has lost both virtue and self-mastery finds their being trapped within the prison of the body and its passions. The unhappiness they feel is the cry of the imprisoned soul calling for its release. The source of happiness is the practice of virtue.

Happiness is the fruit of a decision. Let us decide to be happy and continue to be so, by centering ourselves and maintaining that center, by detaching ourselves from the centrifugal forces of conditioning, distractions, and demands.

Reader, thank you! And to the happiness of being happy!

NOTES

Chapter 1: The Three Crises of Socrates

(1) Administrative division of the ancient Persian Empire.

(2) Cf. Plato, Symposium, 201d-212c.

(3) "Epopteia" (from Greek, meaning "contemplation") refers to the highest degree of initiation in the Mysteries.

(4) Encyclopædia Universalis, article "Socrate et École socratique".

(5) See Plato, Alcibiades, 104e-106a; 119b-130a.

(6) J. Hatzfeld, Alcibiades, p. 57-58. Cited by Françoise Hellmann, Sokratès, Socrate ou la pesée de l'âme, Editions 2&1, p. 157.

(7) Plato, Apology of Socrates, trans. Luc Brisson, Flammarion, p. 109.

(8) Françoise Hellmann, cited work, p. 318.

(9) In the Apology of Socrates, 21c-e, Socrates rejects the offer to cease philosophizing to save his life. We can observe that, for Socrates—without any suicidal tendency—this proposition requires nothing less than renouncing the life of the soul, a loss far more damaging than physical death. However, the true philosopher must not take his own life as that would be impious (cf. Phaedo, 61d and 62a). Here is Socrates' enlightening response: "Let us suppose [that] you were to say to me: 'Socrates, we will not follow the advice of Anytus advice today. We will acquit you instead, on one condition: from now on, pursuing this inquiry, or philosophizing, will not occupy all your time. But if you are caught doing this again, you will die!' If these were the conditions, that you would be willing to acquit me on, I would say to you: 'Athenians, I salute you and love you, but I will obey the god rather than you: until my last breath, as long as I am able, do not expect me to cease philosophizing, to stop addressing you with recommendations, and to point out the truth to anyone I encounter. This is my usual practice: 'O best of men, you who are an Athenian, a citizen of the greatest city, famous for its wisdom and power, yet you are not ashamed to care for wealth, reputation, and honors, while you neglect the thought, truth, and improvement of your soul!' (Apology of Socrates 29c-d).

(10) Cf. Plato, Apology of Socrates, 20e - 21a.

(11) Socrates reflects critically on what has just been said about him. Since the gods do not lie and he himself is aware of his own limitations, he must determine the relevance of the oracle. Here are Socrates' words: "Once I learned of this answer, I thought to myself: 'What can the god mean? What could this riddle possibly signify? For I am not, in any way, aware within myself of being wise! So what does he mean by declaring that I am the wisest of men? Of course, he does not lie, for that is not permitted to him!' For a long time, I was at a loss as to what he could possibly mean, until finally, with much difficulty, I resolved to inquire by proceeding more or less like this. I went to one of those with the greatest reputation for wisdom, convinced that, more than anywhere else, I could refute the response given to Chaerephon and clearly prove to the oracle: 'This man is wiser than I am, yet you declared it of me!' So I undertook a thorough examination of this man (there is no need to name him—he was one of our politicians [referring to Anytus]), and from this examination and our conversation, the impression I received, Athenians, was roughly this: that, in my opinion, this man had, among many others and especially in his own eyes, a reputation for wisdom—but no real wisdom. Then, I endeavoured to show him that while he believed himself wise, he was not. From that moment on, I became odious to him, as well as to many who were listening to our conversation. At least, as I left, I thought to myself: 'Here is a man who is less wise than I am. Indeed, it is possible that neither of us knows anything noble or good. But he believes he knows, while he does not, whereas I, just as I do not actually know, also do not believe that I know! In any case, I seem to be wiser than this man in at least one small respect: namely, that I do not think I know what I do not know!' Following this, I went to another of those whose reputation for wisdom was even greater than that of the previous one. And I had the same experience—another opportunity to make myself odious to him and to many others." (Apology of Socrates, 21bcde).

(12) As indicated in the previous note, Socrates goes on to inquire among those reputed to be wise: politicians (Apology of Socrates, 21c-e), poets (Apology of Socrates, 22a-c), and various craftsmen (Apology of Socrates, 22d-e). His finding is the same everywhere: each person thought themselves wise without a doubt, yet they were not. Moreover, "each of them, because he practiced his art perfectly, believed himself also wise in other matters of the greatest importance. [...] This presumptuous belief overshadowed their other wisdom." (Apology of Socrates, 22b).

(13) See Plato, Apology of Socrates, 21d.

(14) This art of persuasion, of seeking and obtaining the impression of being right, even without reason, perverts language and renders dialogue sterile by making the plausible seem true. This is the source of the real corruption of individuals and the city, and the reign of injustice. In addition to the Protagoras, where Socrates illustrates the dangers of sophists and sophism, we find eloquent examples in The Republic I, 343d-344c. Here Thrasymachus, through masterful sophistic maneuver, attempts to portray injustice as superior to justice due to the apparent advantages and material benefits that it can bring to merchants, taxpayers, and unjust magistrates. The height of sophism is that Thrasymachus essentially

claims that it is the fear of injustice that makes us despise it, not the love of justice.

(15) In Gorgias, 469b-c and 474b-c, Socrates clearly states: "For my part, I would prefer neither one nor the other. But if, inevitably, there were to be either injustice committed or injustice suffered, I would choose to suffer it rather than commit it" (Gorgias, 469c). However, in order to fully understand this Socratic choice, it is necessary to comprehend as Socrates does, the fate of the souls, which in their incarnate condition, allow themselves to commit injustice both toward themselves and toward others. See Phaedo, 107d-115e.

(16) Socrates has always lived by this conviction, teaching it to anyone willing to listen, including his judges. He proves it by refusing the offer of Athenian judges, who told him to stop philosophizing if he wanted to escape the death penalty (cf. Apology of Socrates, 29c-e). Long before that, Socrates refused to commit the injustice of accusing ten generals whom the Council wanted to condemn for failing to retrieve the bodies of Greek soldiers after the naval battle of 406 BCE. He also refused to become an accomplice in the tyranny of the "Thirty" who ordered him and four others to "go to Salamis and bring back Leon the Salaminian, so that he could be executed." (See Apology of Socrates, 32b-d for these events). Elsewhere, Socrates explains why the worst evil is "to hate reasoning" (Phaedo, 89d) or to stop thinking. For it is through thought, irreducible to rational operations, this divine talent, as he calls it in The Republic VII, 519e, that the soul-psyche can free itself from the constraints of the body-soma, free itself of corruptible desires, and take flight, viewing and judging things from a higher perspective, perceiving and experiencing their mutually enriching connection. See Phaedo, 64e; 65acd; 67d; 69c; 79cd; 80b; 81b; 83b for examples.

(17) However, Socrates does not seek to inconvenience anyone. He merely fulfills his task as a philosopher: awakening the consciousness of people so they do not succumb to lethargy and allow themselves to fall into the ease of believing they are excellent when they are mediocre or believing that they know when they are ignorant. See Apology 21d-e, where Socrates acknowledges that from the moment he reveals that those reputed to be wise are not wise at all, he inevitably becomes hated by them and by those who considered them wise and perhaps benefited from their favor by flattering them.

(18) One of the magistrates governing a Greek republic. There were nine in Athens.

(19) Cf. Plato, Apology of Socrates, 28e-29a: "It is God who has assigned me this duty (this is the conviction I had formed), with the obligation to live by philosophizing and examining myself and others. This duty I will not desert for fear of death or anything else."

(20) See Plato, The Republic, IV, 423a-436b.

(21) Plato, Apology of Socrates, 23c-d and 24a.

(22) Plato, ibid.

(23) This is indeed the sentiment reached by the one who, through philosophy, has learned to identify with his soul, which, in contrast to the body that loses both its vigor and tenacity over time, gains in freshness, strength, and swiftness of youth combined with remarkable maturity. This relates to the immortality of the soul, which P.lato discusses in Phaedo, 72e-73a; 76ace; 80a; 87ad; 88a; 91c.

Chapter 2: The Socratic Method

(1) Anne Baudart, Socrate et le socratisme, Armand Colin, p. 87.

(2) This will be developed in Chapter IV.

(3) Pierre Hadot, Éloge de Socrate, Editions Allia, p. 54. Let's recall with Étienne Gilson that "haste fosters the entrenchment of prejudices and opinion within us. Haste is the flaw of forming a judgment before the mind has attained complete evidence. Preconception is the persistence, in our thinking, of thoughtless judgments we made about things during childhood, which now impose themselves upon us as though we had proven them. A judgment held to be true under the influence of preconception is called a prejudice. (Étienne Gilson, in Descartes, Discourse on Method (1637), ed. Jean Vrin, Paris, 1989, second part, note no. 2, p. 69). Before Descartes and Gilson, Socrates had already drawn philosophical attention to the danger of this haste which leads us to mistake shadows for reality in The Republic, VII, and more subtly in examining what is real in Book X of the same work.

(4) Roger Texier, Socrate enseignant, de Platon à nous, Editions L'Harmattan, p. 26.

(5) Pierre Hadot, cited work, p. 54.

(6) This is clearly evident in all of Plato's dialogues where we see Socrates in action. The goal is always to seek, through the illumination of lógos that mediates between interlocutors, the truth that no one holds a monopoly over, but that lies in the space in between, inviting each to approach it and, in doing so, to bring their perception and position closer to those of the other. Thus, as the lógos (word, speech, reason, discourse...) of the other meets my own, we simultaneously become aware of our limitations, our own untapped potential, and that of others. In this sense, truly philosophical dialogue always opens a shared future and a path of convergence for those engaged in it.

(7) To give a few striking examples—since all of Plato's dialogues contain this Socratic art of leading the interlocutor beyond opinions and prejudices in pursuit of truth—it is illustrated in The Symposium concerning the nature of Love, in Meno regarding the nature of Virtue, and in The Republic on the nature of Justice.

(8) See The Republic X, 596ab and 597ab. Reality cannot be reduced to materiality, which often deceives us when we believe we can rely solely on our senses to perceive the real. For reality extends far beyond what is manifested and thus perceptible to our senses. We must often go beyond the phenomenon to come into contact with the idea, the being, or the truth from which the image or sensible materiality originates.

(9) Reason and Thought are not opposed to each other; rather, they operate differently and at varying levels of subtlety, often in a complementary manner. In the diversity of what is manifest—the privileged domain of reason—it is precisely reason that enables us to sort, classify, and organize hierarchically, stacking elements in an order of measurable efficiency. In doing so, it helps us avoid mental confusion and obscurantist mystification. However, it is through thought, by mobilizing intelligence, that we will go beyond rational operations to perceive the meta-rational connections linking what appears separate to our senses —senses that are too limited in their perceptive capacity and too caught up in the immediate will of the moment. In this way, they remain unaware of what Leibniz referred to as the two other wills: the preceding or initial will and the final will (cf. his Theodicy, §119). As long as we have not developed an understanding of these two wills, the connection that unites them with present will—and thus with present reality—will elude us. Consequently, we will perceive contradictions where there is only a harmony in formation, a dialectical relationship between momentary differences, as G.W.F. Hegel illustrates in his Phenomenology of Spirit.

(10) Roger Texier, cited work, p. 138.

(11) Ibidem, p. 139 and 140.

(12) Gregory Vlastos, Socrates: Ironist and Moral Philosopher, Aubier, p. 18/19.

Chapter 3: The Path to Happiness

(1) Gregory Vlastos, Socrates: Ironist and Moral Philosopher, p. 317.

(2) Plato, Symposium, 205a2-3.

(3) Gregory Vlastos, cited work, p. 279.

(4) Ibidem.

(5) Ibidem, p. 318.

(6) Ibidem, p. 303.

(7) Ibidem, p. 318.

Chapter 4: Socratic Pedagogy: Irony

(1) Pierre Hadot, Éloge de Socrate, p. 34.

(2) Friedländer, cited by Pierre Hadot, p. 38.

(3) Pierre Hadot, Ibidem, p. 18.

(4) Ibidem, p. 19.

(5) Ibidem, p. 26.

(6) Gregory Vlastos, cited work, p. 50.

(7) Ibidem, p. 52.

(8) Ibidem, p. 63/64.

Chapter 5: Love According to Socrates

(1) Délia Steinberg Guzman, Course on Metaphysical Aesthetics, p. 3.

(2) Pierre Hadot, Éloge de Socrate, p. 47.

(3) Plato, Symposium, 203 d.

(4) Pierre Hadot, cited work, p. 50.

(5) See Françoise Hellmann, Sokratès, Socrate ou la pesée de l'âme, p. 90/91.

(6) Délia Steinberg Guzman, Course on the History of Ancient Philosophy.

(7) Marcel Détienne, Encyclopædia Universalis, article Orphisme.

(8) Ibidem.

(9) Ibidem.

(10) Yves Dacosta, Initiations et sociétés secrètes dans l'Antiquité gréco-romaine, Berg International Publishers.

(11) Ibidem, p. 65.

(12) W.K.C. Guthrie, Orpheus and Greek Religion, Payot (cited by Yves Dacosta).

(13) Yves Dacosta, cited work, p. 67.

(14) Ibidem, p. 72.

(15) Gregory Vlastos, Socrates: Ironist and Moral Philosopher, p. 226.

(16) Ibidem.

(17) Plato, The Republic, Book II, 379b.

(18) Gregory Vlastos, cited work, p. 230.

(19) Ibidem, p. 244.

(20) Ibidem, p. 245/46.

Conclusion

(1) Anne Baudart, Socrate et le socratisme, p. 40.

CHRONOLOGY

The Life of Socrates and Major Events of the 5th Century BCE in Athens

496 BCE

- Birth of Sophocles, one of the three great Greek playwrights of tragedy, along with Aeschylus (born in 526) and Euripides.

492 BCE

- Beginning of the Greco-Persian Wars: The Persian Empire, already ruling Asian Greece, begins the conquest of European Greece.

490 BCE

- Greek victory over the Persians at Marathon. End of the first Greco-Persian War.

480 BCE

- Birth of Euripides, a friend of Socrates, who the Delphic Oracle will say is a wise man.
- Second Greco-Persian War: invasion and burning of Athens. Crushing victory of the Greek fleet, commanded by Themistocles, at Salamis.

479 BCE

- End of the second Greco-Persian War.
- Beginning of the battles that will drive the Persians out of Asia Minor.
- Hegemony of Athens.

470 BCE

- Birth of Socrates in Athens.

456 BCE

- Death of Aeschylus.

446 BCE

- Birth of Aristophanes, founder of Greek comedy.

444-443 BCE

- Construction of the Temple of Athena on the Acropolis, the Parthenon.

438 BCE

- Erection of the statue (12m high) of Athena, a work of Phidias, in the Parthenon.

432 BCE

- Start of the Peloponnesian War between Sparta and Athens for hegemony.
- Socrates distinguished himself by his bravery at the siege of Potidaea, where he saves Alcibiades' life. This is also where the episode reported in the *Symposium* takes place, when he remains standing in meditation for 24 hours.

430 BCE

- Birth of Xenophon, author, among other things, of works on Socrates.

429 BCE

- The plague devastates Athens. Pericles is among the victims.

428 BCE

- Birth of Plato.

424 BCE

- *The Clouds*, a comedy by Aristophanes, ridicules Socrates.
- Socrates participates in the Battle of Delium where the Athenians are defeated by the Thebans.

422 BCE

- Socrates participates in the campaign at Amphipolis.

420 BCE

- The Oracle of Delphi declares Socrates "the wisest of all men".

414 BCE

- The Sicilian Expedition, led by Alcibiades. Implicated in the scandal of the mutilation of the statues of Hermes, Alcibiades takes refuge in Sparta.

408 BCE

- Return of Alcibiades to Athens.

406 BCE

- Socrates, presiding over the prytany, opposes summary

justice and enforces the law.

- Death of Sophocles and Euripides.

404 BCE

- End of the Peloponnesian War: siege and capitulation of Athens. Collapse of the Athenian Empire. Hegemony of Sparta.
- Assassination of Alcibiades.

404-403 BCE

- Bloody tyranny of the Thirty in Athens.

403 BCE

- Restoration of democracy.

399 BCE

- Denunciation of Socrates, accused of corrupting the youth and impiety. Trial and death of Socrates, condemned to drink hemlock.

BIBLIOGRAPHY

Baudart, Anne, *Socrate et le socratisme*, Armand Colin.

Dacosta, Yves, *Initiations et sociétés secrètes dans l'Antiquité gréco-romaine*, Berg International Éditeurs.

Encyclopædia Universalis, articles *Orphisme, École socratique, Socrate*.

Hadot, Pierre, *Éloge de Socrate*, Éditions Allia.

Hadot, Pierre, *Qu'est-ce que la philosophie antique?*, Folio/Essais, Gallimard. (Available in English as *What is Ancient Philosophy?*)

Hellmann, Françoise, *Sokratès, Socrate ou la pesée de l'âme*, Éditions 2&1.

Plato, *Apology*.

Plato, *Euthyphro*.

Plato, *The Republic*.

Plato, *Symposium*.

Steinberg Guzmán, Délia, Course on *Metaphysical Aesthetics*.

Steinberg Guzmán, Délia, Course on *History of Ancient Philosophy*.

Texier, Roger, *Socrate enseignant, de Platon à nous*, Éditions L'Harmattan.

Vlastos, Gregory, *Socrate, Ironie et philosophie morale*, Aubier. (Available in English as *Socrates: Ironist and Moral Philosopher)*.

ABOUT THE AUTHOR

Fernand Schwarz is the author of numerous works on ancient philosophies and civilizations, particularly on Egypt, including *Ma'at and the Relevance of Ancient Egypt* and *Introduction to the Egyptian Books of the Dead*. He has directed the religious anthropology module at the School of Anthropology in Paris for many years. He contributed to the *Treatise on the Anthropology of the Sacred*, edited by Julien Ries, and he co-produced the film series *Architecture and Sacred Geography*. In 2013, he led the symposium *The Odyssey of Dialectic from Plato to Today*, organized by the International Hermes Institute and the House of Philosophy in Marseille. His profound interest in the philosophical approach to spirituality and its implications for the relationships between humanity, nature, and the spiritual leads him to promote a culture of renaissance, essential for the advent of humanism in the future.

BY THE SAME AUTHOR

AVAILABLE IN ENGLISH:

Concentration & Inner Awakening: According to Tibetan Buddhism. New Acropolis Cultural Organization, India

Perseus – The Warrior of Peace. New Acropolis Cultural Organization, India

AVAILABLE IN FRENCH:

Géographie sacrée de l'égypte ancienne. Éditions Néo

Les traditions de l'amérique ancienne. Editions Dangles

Égypte terre des Dieux, don du Nil. Éditions Nouvelle Acropole

Égypte, les mystères du sacré. Éditions du Félin

Initiation aux livres des morts égyptiens. Éditions Albin Michel

Symbolique de paris. Éditions du huitième jour

Symbolique de l'égypte. Éditions du huitième jour

Symbolique des cathedrals. Éditions du huitième jour

Maât - égypte miroir du ciel. Éditions des 3 Monts

La tradition et les voies de la connaissance. Éditions Nouvelle Acropole

Le totalitarisme ou l'homme denature. Éditions Nouvelle Acropole

Les dangers du racisme. Éditions Nouvelle Acropole

Le symbolisme de l'égypte ancienne et sa géographie sacrée. Éditions Nouvelle Acropole

Le bardo thödol, livre des morts tibétain. Éditions Nouvelle Acropole

Concentration et éveil intérieur selon le bouddhisme tibétain. Éditions Nouvelle Acropole

INTERNATIONAL ORGANIZATION NEW ACROPOLIS

NEW ACROPOLIS

New Acropolis is a worldwide non-profit organization, with centres in over fifty countries.

Established by Professor Jorge Angel Livraga on the foundations of practical philosophy and universal fraternity, New Acropolis is inspired by a fundamental respect for human dignity beyond differences of race, gender, culture, religion or socio-economic status. New Acropolis respects diversity but also tries to transcend it in search of a higher unity through shared universal ethical principles.

At New Acropolis, philosophy is more than just intellectual food for thought. We study philosophy as a means to integrate the sciences, the arts, ethics and metaphysics in order to work towards global human development.

This vision is implemented through a wide range of programmes that combine practical education with cultural and volunteering activities. New Acropolis also promotes an awareness of current affairs, both locally and globally, and focuses on improving the human condition by aligning ourselves with the laws of nature.

To learn more about New Acropolis, **visit www.acropolis.org**